T

*Human Voices of
Prayer and Suffering*

Dedication

I wish to dedicate this book to the team at the Orlagh Centre in Dublin. For the past twelve years it has been my privilege and pleasure to work closely with John Byrne OSA, Lonan Byrne, Seán Goan, John Hughes OSA, Mary Kearney, Kieran O'Mahony OSA, and Bernadette Toal. During that time the team has provided courses, workshops and retreats for people from all over Ireland and beyond. The Centre has become a haven of peace and a place of discovery for many. God grant that its work may continue long into the future.

Carmel McCarthy RSM

'I will sing to the Lord as long as I live.
I will sing praise to my God while I have being.'

Psalm 104:33

The Psalms

*Human Voices of
Prayer and Suffering*

Carmel McCarthy

DOMINICAN PUBLICATIONS

Published (2012) by
Dominican Publications
42 Parnell Square
Dublin 1

ISBN 978-1-905604-18-0

British Library Cataloguing in Publications Data
A cataloguing record for this book is available from the British Library.

Origination by Dominican Publications

Cover and book design by David Cooke

Printed in Ireland by
Naas Printing Ltd
South Main Street
Naas
Co. Kildare

Contents

1 Introduction to Praying with the Psalms

'When you pray, go into your inner room and shut the door and pray to your Father who is in secret' (Matthew 6:6). It is often difficult to find the kind of inner space described in this gospel text. If Jesus were our contemporary today perhaps he might use a different kind of appeal to reach us. We live in a world dominated by consumerism, spin doctors, and a hectic lifestyle. Sound bytes and television advertisements bombard our senses in nonstop succession. Our world is also characterised by war, appalling poverty, starvation, exploitation, and displacement of peoples. All kinds of problems and concerns can overwhelm us, and sidetrack us from making space for God. It is often not possible either physically or metaphorically to 'go into an inner room'. Just as much as people in times past, we too are in need of God and the courage and strength that God's word can give. How can we encounter God in this world of ours today? Can the Psalms teach us pathways to prayer?

A friend once gave me a poster on prayer which I liked so much that I put it in a frame and hung it where I'd see it every day. The poster contained five images of a figure in various emotional states, each accompanied by a different caption: Help! God dammit! Lord have mercy! Thank You! and Wow! The overall heading for the poster was 'All prayers, no matter what the words, are really one of five'. The illustration for Help! depicted a solitary mud-covered hand pushing up out of a mud pool, while that for God dammit! portrayed a little guy with extra-large teeth bared in anger, his clenched hands pulling a cap down over his eyes. When thinking about how these images cleverly illustrate different kinds of prayer, it struck me that they could also be applied broadly speaking to the biblical psalms with somewhat parallel results.

In the following chapters you will find a selection of psalms which hopefully will help you become more attuned to God's presence in today's world and in your personal life. Entering into the different moods of the psalms in a prayerful way can help you to journey into deeper relationship with God. Learning to pray with the psalms will bring you into a dialogue of praise, gratitude, and petition, reflecting your daily circumstances.

You do not pray on your own. You become part of a vast chorus of psalm-users extending back over 2,500 years. So, whether you are on the bus, waiting in a doctor's surgery, walking on a beach, waiting for your baby to wake, sitting in a church or in an 'inner room', this pocket-size book of reflections on the psalms can become a gentle companion to prayer. An added encouragement to pray with the psalms lies in the fact that they were used by Jesus as a young boy growing into adulthood and into his Father's plan for him.

The psalms which follow are grouped under eight different headings. These various groupings may guide you to find a psalm that mirrors in some way your particular need at a given time. Or you may just wish to journey progressively through the book page by page.

Throughout, the focus will be on praying through using the psalms. Each chapter will follow a broadly similar structure. First, you will find a psalm text, occasionally in full, but more often in a shortened form, since many of the psalms are quite long. The translation used throughout is my own, the fruit of over 40 years of teaching biblical Hebrew.[1] Then in a second section some notes on the psalm in question will follow, offering a brief comment on significant words or phrases, as well as an overview of how the psalm unfolds. Third, you will find some suggestions on how you might pray with this particular psalm. The fourth and final section will conclude with a short prayer, incorporating some of the key images and phrases of the psalm.

The overall method of praying with these psalms is very simple. Two steps are recommended: first, an initial reading of the psalm and its accompanying notes, so that you can become more familiar with the flow of the poetry and the psalm's background. This could be described as digging the ground, the preparatory work.

When you are ready, you can take the second step, moving into a quieter phase. This concerns praying itself, the emergence of green shoots of prayer in your heart. After some moments of stillness, of becoming more directly aware of God's presence within you and around you, ask the Holy Spirit to guide you from within. Then read the psalm again, this time slowly and prayerfully. Allow yourself to respond to its beauty, to its images and to its mood. Notice what is

1. Although the historical context of Old Testament times favours the inference that the psalm authors were male, it is reasonable to presume that the influence of women also found its way into the biblical writings which have come down to us. However, since there is no hard evidence in the biblical material for female psalm authors, I have used masculine pronouns throughout, but I invite readers to remain open to the genuine possibility of female authorship in the formulation of some of the psalms. Keeping in mind that God is above gender, I have followed the standard practice of using masculine pronouns relating to God in translating the psalms.

either attractive or not attractive to you. Stay where you feel you are being invited, and only move on when you feel that this is right for you. Some may find it helpful just to pray each word or line very slowly, repeating it gently as seems appropriate. Often, as you become quiet and more tuned into the silence that can envelop you, you may notice how you are being drawn into God's love in a deeper way.

As regards distractions – be patient and smile at them. They are impossible to avoid. Don't fight them. Just come back again to rest gently in the psalm phrase or word that draws you.

Although intended as a pocket-size companion for personal use, this prayer book of psalms can also be used in a *Lectio Divina* group. The usual pattern for *Lectio Divina* could be followed: first, after a suitable moment of quiet, the group leader invites someone to read the psalm text. This is followed by silent reflection, after which participants are invited to echo a word or phrase which has attracted them, without comment. Then the psalm is read aloud a second time, after which some time is given to exploring the text under the guidance of the leader (the psalm notes may be used here). A third reading of the biblical text follows, after which members of the group could share how they find this psalm meaningful for them. The leader then brings the session to a close, perhaps by using the concluding prayer.

2 Please!

Psalms of Petition

Like the outstretched floundering hand of a drowning person, the psalms are full of cries for help. So, let's begin where many a prayer begins, with a cry for help! Each of us knows from personal experience how suddenly chaos and catastrophe can strike, be it bereavement, job loss, financial difficulties, failure in relationships, rejection in its many forms, a doctor's diagnosis. Or it may be nothing more than a sharp word, a disappointment, criticism, or a minor illness. When we turn to these psalms of petition we know we are not alone.

PSALM 13 *Do Not Forsake Me!*

How long, O Lord? Will you utterly forget me?
How long will you hide your face from me?
How long must I bear conflict in my soul,
grief in my heart day after day?
How long will my enemy triumph over me?

Look! Answer me, O Lord my God!
Give light to my eyes, lest I sleep in death,
lest my enemy say, 'I have overcome him';
lest my foes rejoice because I stumble.

As for me, in your faithful love I trust,
let my heart rejoice in your salvation.
Let me sing to the Lord,
because he has been good to me.

NOTES ON PSALM 13

How long? This question is repeated four times in the opening lines. The repetition draws out the author's sense of isolation and abandonment. It may mean that the psalmist has undergone many days, perhaps even years of suffering.

utterly forget me: Literally, 'forget me forever'. The psalmist feels totally forgotten and abandoned. Perhaps there is even a suggestion of feeling rejected? That God should 'forget' is inconceivable, as Isaiah 49:15 reminds us: 'Can a woman forget her infant, or be without tenderness for the child of her womb? Even should she forget, I will never forget you.'

hide your face: The experience of God's 'face' being 'hidden' is a recurrent theme in the psalms. This metaphor includes the many different ways in which people can experience God's absence. It also conveys the mysterious nature of this hidden God, this Being who cannot ever be fully understood or controlled by our limited minds and hearts.

conflict: The word here means 'rebellion', rather than just 'pain' or 'sorrow'. The psalmist finds it difficult to accept the current situation and even fights against it.

grief: The sense here is that of the distress that follows anxiety and turmoil of spirit.

my enemy: The 'enemy' here and elsewhere in the psalms is almost always anonymous. We never know exactly to whom the psalmist is referring. This quality of anonymity allows for many different kinds of 'enemy', according to the different needs of those praying the psalm. The 'enemy' may be outside me, with a name and address. We can take some comfort here from seeing how difficulties in relationships have always been present in human interaction, and how they can be a painful source of turmoil. But equally the 'enemy' may be within. How often do we acknowledge that we are 'our own worst enemy'? The conflict and grief of the earlier lines are linked with the 'enemy'. The speaker is not necessarily placing all the blame at the enemy's feet, but turns to God for help in dealing with the conflict.

Look! Answer me!: The psalmist is not afraid to issue God with orders. Both verbs are imperatives.

give light: This could mean either to 'restore lustre' to my eyes (after protracted weeping), or 'to enlighten' internally so that I can really appreciate that, even in my distress, God is on my side.

lest: This word is repeated three times, as if to emphasise the dire consequences that will come about if God does not come to the help of the psalmist.

sleep in death: This could mean total annihilation, since belief in an afterlife was not yet well developed in the Old Testament. To be overcome by 'the enemy' would then be seen as being utterly forsaken by God, an unthinkable disaster.

my foes: Here you will notice that the psalmist uses a typical Hebrew poetic feature called 'parallelism', that of rhyming ideas rather than rhyming words. In simple terms, the poet seems to be saying the same thing twice for greater effect, so that here 'foes' and 'enemy' are in parallelism with each other, and lie at the heart of one and the same conflict that is being experienced.

faithful love: These two words translate one Hebrew word, *hesed*, which is most often used in the Bible to describe God's love relationship with ancient Israel (and by extension, God's love for us today too). This word *hesed* is so full of meaning that no single English word can capture and translate all its richness. It includes God's mercy, tenderness and compassion, covenant faithfulness, loyalty, in sum God's enduring steadfast love. It occurs very often in the psalms.

Let my heart rejoice: The psalmist ends with an invitation to rejoice and sing, out of gratitude for having been delivered by God from distress and suffering.

salvation: The proper name Joshua comes from this word. In its Greek form, it is the name Jesus, who as Saviour is the one who rescues and saves us.

Suggestions for Praying with Psalm 13

There are three parts or movements in Psalm 13, each of which can help you to pray when in distress. First, there is a pleading with God to look upon you in your distress. With the psalmist you can ask if God is really going to remain hidden and oblivious to your pain or anxiety. You can rightly ask 'How long?' Whatever is causing you pain or suffering is experienced as 'your enemy'. Stay as long as seems helpful with these first four lines, moving from word to word, lingering wherever you feel attracted. Allow yourself to feel 'God-forsaken' in your suffering, and continue to ask God, 'How long?'

In the second movement, with the psalmist, speak directly to God, 'Look! Answer me!' Ask for the grace to be enlightened, to be able to see that what you are anxious about has a part to play in God's larger picture. Pray that your 'enemies', that is, your problem or the source of your suffering, can in God's providence become more bearable. Stay with this petition as long as you can, again using the words of the psalm. Return to these lines often, praying for yourself or for those whom you love. The journey through pain is often very long, and at times without an apparent end in sight.

Finally, in the third movement, there is a change in tone or mood, as the psalmist expresses trust in this hidden God. It may take time and courage to enter into this third movement, especially if your suffering continues. But be patient, trusting that you will reach a point where you will be able to accept and enter more fully into God's faithful love for you – even if this means more suffering This psalm could also be prayed in the spirit of Jesus' suffering, death and resurrection, with the first part linked to Good Friday, the second to Holy Saturday, and the third to Easter Sunday.

Concluding Prayer

Amazing God, you never cease to care
    for me in my hour of need.
You know my distress and, although you seem hidden,
you come to give me courage in my darkest hours.
Teach me to recognise your presence in the midst of
    suffering.
Enable me to seek moments of silence
so that I can experience more deeply your faithful love
in the details of my very ordinary life.
Within the loving and healing arms of Jesus,
I make this prayer. Amen.

PSALM 31   *Set Me Free!*

In you, O Lord, I take shelter,
never let me be put to shame.
In your justice set me free!
Bend your ear to me! Hasten to deliver me!

Be a rock of strength for me,
a walled fortress to save me.
For you are my rock and my rampart,
for your name's sake lead me and guide me.

Pull me out of the net they have hidden for me,
for you are my stronghold.
Into your hand I commend my spirit,
you have rescued me, Lord, God of truth.

You who have seen my misery,
and know the distress of my soul,

you have not handed me over to the enemy,
but have set my feet in a broad place.

Be gracious to me, Lord,
for I am in trouble.
With grief my eye wastes away,
my soul and body also.

My life is worn out through sorrow,
my years through groaning.
My strength fails through misery,
my limbs waste away.

But I trust in you, Lord,
I say, 'You are my God'.
Let your face shine on your servant.
Save me in your faithful love.

NOTES ON PSALM 31

be put to shame: The psalmist asks that his trust in the Lord may never
become a cause for ridicule or dishonour. This could happen in two
possible ways: (i) the psalmist's enemies could scoff at him because they
interpret his trust as naïve or ill-founded; (ii) the psalmist himself may
be tempted to doubt the Lord, and so prays that such a dishonourable
thing may never happen.

justice: When the Bible speaks of God's justice, it understands it not as 'an
eye for an eye' but as essentially linked to God's mercy, and grounded in
God's love for humankind.

your name's sake: God's name occurs often in the psalms. In biblical terms it stands for God's very being, for what we would say in

today's language: the very person of God. That is why one of the Ten Commandments forbids the taking of God's name in vain, since doing so was seen as a direct insult to the very essence of God.

set me free: The verb here commonly describes the act of rescuing a person from danger or an animal from a snare.

set me free! bend! hasten! These three verbs are expressed as imperatives! As in Psalm 13, here too the psalmist is not afraid to issue commands to God!

bend your ear: The psalms often portray God as having eyes, ears, hands. They describe God as bending down to listen, and tell of our being held in God's hand. These biblical metaphors are very powerful ways of deepening our awareness of God's closeness, because they speak of words and actions familiar to us. Thus, our search for God is expressed in human language which is full of symbols. The Bible invites us to use these symbols as stepping stones into the mystery of a loving God who is greater than anything our human language can express. God has given us only one enduring Word in this respect, Jesus.

a rock of strength: This figure, which has become part of everyday language, is further strengthened by the parallel images of a walled fortress and a stronghold.

pull me: The Hebrew verb used here means literally 'bring me up out of'. The psalmist begs God to be pulled free from being entangled in the net that some unnamed enemies have laid for him.

Into your hand I commend my spirit: The psalmist surrenders himself into God's loving hand, even though terrorised by enemy snares. This line is familiar to us because it is placed on Jesus' lips on the cross in Luke 23:46. The context of Jesus' suffering and death at the hands of 'enemies' thus becomes a most eloquent and dramatic fulfilment of the psalmist's surrender in the midst of persecution. This verse is also echoed by Stephen, the first Christian martyr, as he too dies at the hands of evildoers (Acts 7:59).

misery ... distress: These words are used interchangeably here, a further example of how parallel ideas rhyme in the psalms. The main point in these lines, however, is that God sees the psalmist's distress and God knows. God's compassionate awareness is the source of the psalmist's trust, in spite of much suffering.

not handed me over: God will never hand the suffering person over into the control of 'the enemy'. This verb has the basic sense of 'to shut someone in'.

a broad place: In contrast to being 'shut in', God will provide the petitioner with the freedom and security of 'broad open spaces'.

Be gracious to me: The verb used here means 'to feel sympathy for, to have pity on'.

in trouble: This image describes what being in trouble feels like: it is 'to be in a narrow place', the opposite to a broad place of the previous line.

wastes away: A number of images of distress now follows, as the psalmist describes why God should take pity on him: he is wasting away, worn out, groaning, and has failing strength.

Let your face shine: In spite of anguish and distress, the psalm ends on a trusting note. The psalmist asks yet again that God take note of his petition, as he appeals this time to experience some sense of God's presence and faithful love.

Suggestions for Praying with Psalm 31

As in the case of Psalm 13, this psalm is also a plea to God for help in time of need. Here too the precise nature of the need is not clear, but this is not essential. This lack of precision makes it possible for us today to enter more personally into the movement of the psalm, so as to allow its pleas to become ours. The psalm contains a sense of being trapped, which alternates with pleas for deliverance and a longing to be set free from suffering of soul and/or body. These pleas are grounded in an over-arching trust, where God is experienced as a strong rock and a trustworthy guide.

This is a psalm which can be prayed almost daily, as we are seldom without some kind of suffering or personal anxiety. We can also pray this psalm when concerned about the suffering of those whom we love. There are many ways in which we can feel trapped, and there are many ways in which we need to be set free. The trust that lies at the heart of this psalm is summed up in the verse placed on the lips of Jesus as he surrenders his life to his Father: 'Into your hands I commend my spirit' (Luke 23:46). As you move to and fro gently through this psalm, linger where you feel attracted, and where you find your trust and faith strengthened.

Concluding Prayer

Compassionate and tender-hearted God of mercy,
be gracious to me in my hour of grief.
Pull me out of the nets that lie hidden in my path.
Bend your ear to me and lift me out of my darkness.
When my courage fails through distress,
be a rock of strength for me.
Even if my life seems worn out through sorrow,
let me always trust in you, O Lord.
Into your hands I commend my spirit.
This prayer I make beneath the cross of Jesus, my
   Saviour. Amen.

PSALM 55   *A Plea for Respite*

God, pay heed to my prayer!
Do not hide yourself from my pleading!
Listen to me and answer me!
I shudder in my grief, I am in panic.

My heart writhes within me,
the terrors of death assault me.

Fear and trembling invade me,
shuddering overwhelms me.

I say, 'If only I had wings like a dove
that I might fly away and find rest.

Indeed, far away I would flee,
I would lodge in the wilderness.
There I would quickly find respite
from the raging wind and tempest.'

Cast your burden upon the Lord,
and he will sustain you.
God will never let the righteous collapse.
As for me, I put my trust in you.

NOTES ON PSALM 55

pay heed: The verb used here implies a careful listening: 'give ear'. This
   need for assurance that God is really taking careful note of the poet's
   plea is reinforced in the third line, with 'listen'.

my pleading: The pleading here is parallel with 'prayer' in the first line.
   This means that, for the psalmist, as much as for us, a recurring form of
   prayer involves pleading or petition.

shudder: The Hebrew verb used here conveys the agitation and anxiety of
   the speaker as he begins to list the reasons for his pleading.

in panic: The literal sense of the verb used here is 'to be out of one's senses,
   to go wild'. To be 'in panic' is a modern equivalent of the agitation and
   distress evoked in this line.

My heart writhes: The image underlying the Hebrew verb here evokes
   the pains of childbirth, and describes the psalmist's immense anguish.
   This torment is reinforced by the rest of the verse, with its images of
   deadly terror, fear, trembling and shuddering.

wings like a dove: Children of all ages are fascinated by the freedom of a
bird in flight. The poet longs for this kind of freedom – to able to fly far
from his current anguish of body and spirit. He seeks a breathing space
in the wilderness, which in certain biblical images is not so much an arid
wasteland as a place of simplicity, without distractions or false promises
or 'the malicious whisperings of the enemy'.

lodge: Here the sense is of a temporary stay of one or two nights, to recu-
perate before returning to resume the business of life with renewed
energy and vision.

respite: The psalmist's desire for flight is not one of escape, but rather a
necessary 'time out' to gain perspective on current distress.

raging wind and tempest: These are vivid images which are often used
symbolically in the psalms to describe the assaults of the 'enemy'. These
enemy onslaughts could be physical or psychological.

Cast your burden: These words express how the psalmist has made a long
journey from feeling immense distress at the beginning of the psalm to
a solid conviction that God stands ready to help. The invitation to cast
your burden upon the Lord who will sustain you, is echoed in Jesus'
invitation, 'Come to me, all you who labour and are burdened, and I
will give you rest' (Matthew 11:28).

I put my trust in you: Notwithstanding how much the psalmist has had
to suffer, he finally reaches a point where he can say, no matter how
tentatively, that God will not let him collapse.

Suggestions for Praying with Psalm 55

This psalm is also a plea to God for help in time of need. The
language is direct and expresses raw human fear and anxiety in the midst of stress. The poet is very forthcoming on
what it feels like to panic and to be in need of urgent help.
Although he does not specify exactly the cause of his distress,
it is clear that he is at his wits' end, and almost in a stupor,
writhing, trembling and shuddering.

There are times in our lives when we undergo panic, and come close to the experience described in the first part of this psalm. Thus, it can be helpful in our times of stress and uncertainty to turn to this psalm, and to pray slowly through it by staying with each word and each line, repeating various words as seems appropriate. It may be difficult to do this, as the very nature of panic means that we are in turmoil and may find it difficult to focus. But by trying to relax and to stay with the psalm's words and imagery, we can be helped to calm our anxiety and become gradually more open to the kind of trust that the psalmist expresses at the end.

A psalm like this one gives us confidence in making prayerful petition. We must not be afraid to bring our needs directly to God, and to plead for some relief and means to hold firm in the midst of what may feel like a hurricane or tsunami. With the psalmist we can ask 'for wings like a dove' to fly to a safe place to shelter during the worst of the storm. And, when the brunt of the blizzard has passed, we may reach that point where we can 'cast our burden on the Lord', knowing that God is the One in whom alone we can find true rest.

Concluding Prayer

Great caring God of mercy, strength and peace,
bend your listening ear to my cry for help.
When fear and trembling invade me
be at my side to strengthen me.
Give me wings like a dove
that I may fly into your loving arms,
and there find courage to face the storms of life.
Teach me to cast my burdens upon you,
knowing that you await me with love and understanding.
This I pray through Jesus, your Son. Amen.

PSALM 71   *A Prayer in Later Years*

My God, deliver me from the hand of the wicked,
from the clutch of the unjust and the lawless.
You are my hope, Lord,
my trust, O Lord, from my youth.

On you I have leaned since my birth,
you took me from my mother's womb.
My mouth is filled with your praise,
and with your splendour all day long.

Do not cast me aside in my old age,
nor abandon me as my strength fails.
For my enemies speak against me,
those with designs on my life are plotting together.

God, you have taught me from my youth,
and I am still proclaiming your marvels.
Now that I am old and grey-haired, O God, do not
    abandon me,
till I have proclaimed your strength to generations yet
    to come.

From the depths of the earth,
you will bring me up again.
You will restore my honour,
and comfort me once more.

I will praise you with the lyre
for your faithfulness, my God,
and sing praises to you with the harp,
O Holy One of Israel!

NOTES ON PSALM 71

deliver me: This plea to God to be delivered is frequent in psalms of petition (see Psalm 31 above), and is often poetically balanced with an appeal to be rescued.

hand of the wicked: The word 'hand' in this opening line symbolises being in the enemy's power. To be in someone's power means to be clutched or grasped in a tight hold, with no room for manoeuvre. This is how the psalmist feels, and begs for release.

hope … trust: These words reinforce each other, as the speaker places all his hope and trust in God.

from my youth: It becomes clear, as the psalm unfolds, that the experience of a lifetime is being condensed.

I have leaned: God has been the mainstay of this person's life, the One to whom the speaker has repeatedly turned for support.

since my birth: Literally, 'from the womb'. The poet is acknowledging God's support as having been present even before birth. This fact becomes clearer in the parallelism of the next line, which describes God as a midwife, ensuring a safe delivery.

You took me: The Hebrew verb here is 'to cut', evoking the symbolism of cutting the umbilical cord.

filled with your praise: Such divine care and providence in the poet's personal life story calls for an outpouring of praise lasting all day long.

cast me aside: The verb which the poet chooses here has the sense of 'to discard, get rid of something for which one no longer has any use'. There is pathos in this plea coming from a person who has been a loyal and faithful servant of God throughout a long life.

nor abandon me as my strength fails: The pathos becomes even stronger in this line through the use of the verb 'abandon'. This same verb occurs in Psalm 22:1 ('My God, my God, why have you abandoned me?'). At a time in the poet's life when he would have hoped for greater support as his strength fails, he pleads with God not to abandon him.

For my enemies speak against me: The reason for the plea becomes clear. The psalmist is at the mercy of plotting and scheming enemies who are ready to kill if necessary.

from my youth: Once again the poet reminds God of a long life lived in faithful trust, a life in which he wants to proclaim God's marvels to the very end. As an old and grey-haired servant, he pleads once more that God not abandon him.

strength: The Hebrew word used here is 'arm', a common biblical symbol for God's power and strength.

to generations yet to come: This poet wants to remain faithful to the very end so that his trust in God can reach beyond his own life span.

From the depths of the earth you will bring me up again: The poet trusts that God's providential love will rescue him from the depths of the darkness he experiences, and that he will be restored to his former good standing. Belief in a personal resurrection after death would not have been part of the original psalmist's plea. But this does not prevent us from praying this mysterious line as a foreshadowing of our Christian belief in personal resurrection.

comfort me once more: The psalmist ends on a confident note that, having gone through these many trials, God will again comfort and console him in the here and now, and so the psalmist will be able to sing praises to God once again with joyful heart.

Suggestions for Praying with Psalm 71

Although the speaker in this psalm appears to be an elderly person, this does not mean that the psalm cannot be profitably used by a younger person. The experience of needing to be freed from the power of 'enemy forces' is one that can occur from teenage years onward.

The mood of the psalm alternates between petition to be delivered from the power of such 'enemies', and expressions of trust, praise and thanksgiving. The psalmist pleads twice not to be abandoned by God whose guiding providence he has experienced since his earliest memories. He speaks of being in the clutch of the lawless, an experience that is as fearful as being exposed to those plotting to kill him. But he is equally forthright in his praise and gratitude for having God by his side from his youth to the present.

There are times in our lives when we may feel abandoned and fearful for various reasons. We may lack strength as we advance in years and health issues become as potent as 'enemies'. At such times the feelings of the psalmist may help us, as the mood of the psalm moves from fear to trust and back again to fear. Here too, it may help if we move gently through the psalm, lingering where we find help. We notice that the psalmist makes a journey from petition to praise that can mirror changes in our inner landscape.

Concluding Prayer

Wonderful, caring and nurturing God,
faithful companion through life's journey,
keep me close by your side for my remaining time on
    earth.
You have been with me since my youth,
even though I have often forgotten to be with you.
Pull me towards wholeness,
unclutter my mind of useless chatter.
Now that the evening of life draws closer
set me free from useless anxiety.
Watch over those I love and who are precious to me.
I pray in the name of Jesus my Saviour and lifetime
    Friend. Amen.

3 Help!

Psalms of Frustration

In the previous chapter we examined four psalms of petition, with their focus on various situations in which the psalm authors cry to God for help. The psalms at the centre of this chapter are also psalms of petition, but this time their focus is on the intensity of frustration experienced, which the psalmist is not afraid to express directly to God. This is something that some modern people may find difficult if not impossible – to bring feelings of anger to God in prayer. But there are places in these ancient prayers where the psalmists 'get it off their chest' so to speak, and take God to task! The first of these psalms, Psalm 22, will be divided into two parts, on account of its length, and its significance in the Christian tradition.

PSALM 22 (I) *A Prayer in Deep Distress*

> My God, my God, why have you abandoned me?
> Why so far from delivering me?
> From the words of my screaming?
>
> My God, I cry by day, but you do not answer,
> by night, and I have no respite.
> Yet you are holy,
> you who inhabit the praises of Israel.
>
> In you our ancestors trusted,
> they trusted and you rescued them.

To you they cried out and were rescued,
in you they trusted and were not disappointed.

But I am a worm, less than human,
scorned by everyone, despised by people.

All who see me jeer at me.
They curl their lips, they shake their heads:
'He relied on the Lord – let him rescue him!
Let him deliver him, since he took delight in him.'

Yet it was you who drew me from the womb,
made me secure at my mother's breast.
Upon you was I cast from birth,
from my mother's womb you have been my God.

NOTES ON PSALM 22 (I)

why have you abandoned me?: The opening line of Psalm 22 is so familiar
to Christians that it is difficult not to think of these words as uniquely
those of Jesus on the cross. But first let us remember that this psalm
had a long life before its initial line was placed on Jesus' lips in Luke's
account of the passion. The psalm begins with this cry from the heart,
and sets the tone for the anguish which will follow as the psalm unfolds.

from delivering me: The word here is 'my salvation', that is, 'my need to
be saved'.

my screaming: The word chosen by the psalmist is from a Hebrew verb
which usually describes a lion's roar, or the scream of a person in pain.
These first three lines set the mood of the psalm as one in which the
psalmist feels so utterly abandoned, that he cannot but scream in
torment as he pleads with God, questioning why God allows him to
be in this anguished, abandoned state. We may not feel comfortable in
reading these lines which express anger, particularly as this may conflict

with our understanding of Jesus' surrender in love to his Father on the cross. This is a question to which we will return further below.

by day ... by night: The plight of the poet is all-encompassing – there is no 'respite', no period of time when his torment can be forgotten.

no respite: The word chosen by the psalmist means 'silence' or 'quiet'. This may refer to the ongoing crying and screaming in pain that is his continual plight, from which there is no moment of quiet.

who inhabit the praises of Israel: The poet uses this idiom to describe Israel's sense of divine presence accompanying their psalm-singing during temple worship. He cannot believe that God, who is all holy, and the One to whom Israel continually offers praise, can allow this suffering to continue.

our ancestors trusted: There is poignancy in the contrast between the poet's desperate plight and the repeated way in which he reminds God of the trust his ancestors have shown in the past.

a worm: A biblical symbol of something lowly and worthless, it could also represent death, since from the Bible's perspective human beings in the end are consumed by worms. Here the psalmist is hinting at being a cast-off, as good as dead.

jeer at me: The taunting here and throughout this verse shows how bitterly the poet feels his plight. The very source of his hope, his trust in God, is being tossed back at him to compound his desolation. These lines were understood by the early Christians as prophetic descriptions of the taunting undergone by Jesus in his passion, and they continue to be integrated into the liturgy of passion week.

you who drew me from the womb: Here, as in Psalm 71 above, God is described as a midwife, present in the poet's life story from birth. The entire verse is a powerful statement of how the psalmist affirms that, no matter how he may be taunted, God indeed has been present from the first moments of life to the present crisis.

Upon you was I cast from birth: Continuing the imagery of a divine midwife, the psalmist makes it clear that he has no choice but to insist that he belongs only to God.

Suggestions for Praying with Psalm 22 (1)

From earliest years we've been told that it's not nice to be angry. It's not Christian to talk about frustration and anger when praying. But the psalmist does. The psalmist is a realist. The psalmist knows what we are reluctant to admit. We have moments of anger, moments of frustration and moments that are embarrassing (at least to ourselves, if not also to others). And often we don't know what to do about it. Such moments are not unlike the cartoon drawing of a little guy with extra-large teeth bared in anger, his clenched hands pulling a cap down over his eyes, and the caption God dammit! underneath him. Have you ever felt like that? And what do you typically do, when you admit that this happens?

The psalmist turns to God in his pain and distress. Allow the words of the psalmist to become yours, praying each line slowly. Allow yourself to admit how you really feel. Do not be afraid to do this. If you feel abandoned, if you feel rejected by others, if you feel the object of scorn or calumny, if you feel misunderstood, bring these feelings to God in prayer. Notice that the psalmist gradually reaches a point of expressing trust that, in spite of his frustration and pain, he nevertheless knows that God has been with him since birth, and will continue to be there for him. Can you accept that this is true for you also?

Now, in a second stage, pray this psalm with Jesus on the cross. In the passion narrative of Luke the opening words of this psalm are placed on Jesus' lips. They convey the sense of awful dereliction experienced by Jesus in his passion. As the psalm unfolds, we can try to feel with Jesus the rejection and scorn heaped upon him. We can also pray to reach a point of acceptance as Jesus did, knowing that God's love is greater than any experience of pain, rejection or isolation in the here and now.

Concluding Prayer

Ever-present God of compassion,
do not abandon me as I cry to you for help.
Walk by my side in my time of distress.
You, who have been with me since before my birth,
calm my anxious heart.
Help me to remember that I belong to you.
Under the shadow of the cross of Jesus
I make this prayer in union with him
who was faithful to you until death. Amen.

PSALM 22 (II) *A Prayer in Deep Distress*

This second section of Psalm 22 is like a mirror image of
the first. Here too, the psalmist moves from descriptions of
extreme distress to expressions of trust in God's saving help.
This psalm was especially important to the early Christian
community. This can be seen in the fact that the casting
of lots for Jesus' garments, recorded by all four evangelists
(Matthew 27:35; Mark 15:24; Luke 23:34; John 19:23-24), was
seen as a fulfilment of the Scriptures (Psalm 22:19).

Do not stay far from me, for trouble is near,
and there is none to help.
Like water my life drains away.
All my bones are disjointed.

My heart has become like wax,
it melts away within me.
My mouth is as dry as earthenware,
my tongue sticks to my jaw.
You lay me down in the dust of death.

For dogs are all around me,
a pack of evildoers encircles me.
So shrivelled are my hands and feet
that I can count all my bones.

They stare at me and gloat.
They divide my clothes among them,
and for my garments they cast lots.

But you, LORD, do not be far away.
O my strength, come quickly to help me.
Deliver me from the sword,
my one and only life from the clutches of the dog.

Then I will proclaim your name to the assembly,
praising you in the midst of the community.

NOTES ON PSALM 22 (II)

trouble: The underlying image here is that of being confined in a narrow
space from which escape is virtually impossible.

Like water: Water in the Bible is a symbol of life. Where water is absent
there is desert, and absence of life. Water draining into the ground is an
apt image of a life draining away.

disjointed: The verb here refers to bones becoming separated or dislocated from one another. This image of dislocated bones begins a series
of ways in which the poet feels completely ruined and in need of divine
help.

like wax: The fragile remains of the honeycomb is an metaphor for anxiety eating away one's strength or resolve.

dry as earthenware: The image here and in the line immediately following conveys the effects of terror.

dogs: All references to dogs in the Bible are negative. Dogs were never seen as domestic pets; they were on the same level as animals of prey, such as wolves.

pack of evildoers: The image is now more concrete and applied to the 'enemies' as though they were a marauding pack.

count all my bones: This is a very dramatic description of the psalmist's plight, a description often used later by Christians in contemplating Jesus' sufferings on the cross.

They divide my clothes ... for my garments they cast lots: The depths of humiliation and shame to which the author of these lines has been brought in his suffering was seen by all four evangelists as prophetically fulfilled in Jesus' passion.

do not be far away: In spite of his awful plight, the psalm author ends on a note of trust as he appeals to God to be near him, to help him, to deliver him from the dangers he sees closing in on him.

My one and only life: It is difficult to translate the original text here, as it contains a number of nuances in its choice of words. The adjective comes from a Hebrew word for 'one'. This adjective was used to describe Abraham's only son, Isaac, whom he loved (Genesis 22:2). Here it could be rendered as 'my unique life' or 'my one and only life' or 'my precious life'.

proclaim your name: The speaker acknowledges that God alone is to be praised and thanked, even if the circumstances are difficult and the experience heartbreaking. As in the earlier psalms explored above, there is a long journey evoked here, a journey from desolation and pain to acceptance and praise. It presupposes a growth in insight that may take many years.

Suggestions for Praying with Psalm 22 (II)

This psalm, like many others, contains feelings of anger and frustration. The speaker has no one to turn to except God, and tries to understand his feelings in the process.

We too, like the psalmist, often experience anger. Anger is an honest reaction to the cost of pain, but we may not realise this as we have often been programmed to hide our anger or deny that it exists. Anger, if not acknowledged and channeled in a healthy way, can lead to revenge. Because the psalms can and do speak openly of anger and enemies, they provide an outlet for channeling anger. They don't explain anger away, but they do provide graphic images and metaphors that resonate with our lives. The value of anger is that it can help us to understand ourselves better.

When we are angry we can do one of three things: we can explode, or we can swallow anger and allow it to poison us, or we can articulate why we are upset, and explore what is going on in ourselves instead of continuing to concentrate on the other person (as 'enemy'). I can do nothing to change the other, but I can do something about myself. Mark Twain once said that 'anger is an acid that can do more harm to the vessel in which it is stored than to anything on which it is poured'. A psalm, such as this one, which speaks of the reality of anger and enemies can help us recognise these powerful emotions in our own lives.

Thus, it can be a good and healing experience to try to enter into your hidden feelings of anger as you let the verses of this psalm become part of your prayer. Allow yourself to feel the pain of the psalmist first, and then allow points of contact with your experience to emerge. Finally, in a third moment, turn to Jesus in his passion and ask for the grace to accept your pain in union with his.

Concluding Prayer

Almighty God of creation and eternity,
do not stay far from me when trouble is near.
Allow my unique life to discover its true meaning

within your caring providence.
Be near me when my courage falters,
when my emotions are raw and threaten to overwhelm
    me.
Calm me, comfort me, forgive me.
Be my strength and source of truth.
Within the loving and healing arms of Jesus
I make this prayer. Amen.

PSALM 37   *The Contradictions of Life*

Do not be angry because of evildoers,
nor incensed by those who do wrong.
Like grass they shrivel up quickly,
like green plants they wither away.

Trust in the Lord and do good,
that you may dwell in the land and enjoy security.
Delight yourself in the Lord
and he will grant you your heart's desires.

Commit your way to the Lord.
Trust in him, and he will act.
Be still before the Lord,
and wait patiently for him.

Do not be angry over the prosperous,
or over one who plots wicked schemes.
Refrain from anger and abandon wrath.
Do not be angry, it only leads to trouble.

A little while and the wicked will be no more,
however carefully you search for their place, they will
    not be there.
Better the little of the just person
than the great wealth of the wicked.

The wicked person borrows but does not pay back,
but the just person is generous in giving.
God's teaching is in his heart.
A peaceful person can look forward to the future.

NOTES ON PSALM 37

Do not be angry: The speaker addresses an unidentified listener, perhaps
even himself! The verbs are in the second person singular.

incensed: The usual meaning of the verb is 'to be jealous of', but in this
context, in parallel with 'be angry', a more suitable rendering is 'to be
filled with rage against'.

Like grass ... like green plants: Both lines reinforce the message beneath
the imagery: as green shoots have an extremely short lifespan in the dry
climate of semi-desert land, so too the fate of the wicked.

Trust in the Lord and do good: The advice given here is likewise to an
unidentified person, encouraging him or her to remain faithful.

and enjoy security: The verb used here normally means 'to pasture', and
the noun means 'fidelity' or 'loyalty'. The resulting image is that of sheep
securely grazing in familiar and reliable surroundings.

Delight yourself in the Lord: A life lived in integrity will bring its own
peace, echoing the traditional proverb that 'virtue is its own reward'.

Commit: The Hebrew verb here is one that conveys the image of 'rolling
up' a scroll or a document, a symbol of deciding on a course of action.

Trust in him: Instead of being perturbed or frustrated about the actions
of evildoers, the psalmist urges the listeners to entrust themselves to
God.

Be still: Or 'be silent'.

wait patiently: Although the verb means 'to wait', the nuance of its gram-
matical form here is best translated as 'waiting with patience'.

Do not be angry: The psalm author repeats the opening advice about
not getting into a futile and frustrating state of anger against evildoers,
advice which is repeated again at the end of this verse.

the prosperous: It is clear from the context, especially the next two lines,
that here it is not a case of honest prosperity, but of that gained through
evil scheming.

it only leads to trouble: This is practical advice, gained from observing
what can happen in life. The word 'trouble' could also be rendered as
'evil', indicating that the outcome of giving way to anger could bring a
person into a morally blameworthy situation.

A little while and the wicked will be no more: This observation, reinforced by the line which follows, comes from a biblical tradition of
proverbial wisdom gleaned over years of experience. While this proverb
may be true in many instances, there are also painful exceptions, as the
story of Job illustrates.

Better the little of the just person: Another proverbial observation, which
continues the wisdom theme of this psalm.

does not pay back: This is a typical situation, born of long experience. It
is counterbalanced by the corresponding portrait of the generosity of
the just.

God's teaching: This could also be rendered as 'God's law'. This is the
motivation of the just person's generosity, a desire to faithfully follow
God's teaching as expressed in the Scriptures.

the future: This word, which can mean 'outcome' or 'end time', has
been interpreted more concretely in some translations as 'offspring' or
'posterity'.

Suggestions for Praying with Psalm 37

This psalm approaches anger in a different way from the
psalms explored above. Its opening lines come from a

position of trust in God, and express the conviction that a life of evildoing is futile. The psalm author is like a wise teacher, giving advice to an apprentice on the best way to deal with the contradictions and injustices of life: 'Do not be angry because of evildoers', the poet says, because, 'like grass they shrivel up quickly.' Further on the psalmist reaffirms a position of trust: 'Be still before the Lord, and wait patiently', advising his student to 'refrain from anger', as 'it only leads to trouble'.

This advice reflects the received opinion of the psalmist's time, when exploitation of good-living people was often met by simply more exploitation and injustice.

Not much has changed in this regard over the centuries. While today there are greater opportunities to obtain legal aid to defend against injustice and aggression, there are still too many ways in which the vulnerable are exploited and oppressed, while evildoers continue their dishonest schemes unchallenged and unpunished.

There are various ways in which this psalm can become part of your prayer. You may have been – or currently are – the victim of corrupt schemes, either on a large or a small scale. Having done what is in your power to take appropriate action, you can bring all of the anger, pain and uncertainty of this experience to God in prayer, as the psalmist has done before you.

Allow the different lines of the psalm to speak to your painful situation. If you have come through a bad experience, you may be able to pray especially with the psalm's words of confidence and peace, thanking God for his help and support. Or you might pray this psalm with someone else in mind, someone close to you who has been wrongfully cheated or harmed. Or you may identify with those who suffer in the many places of conflict and strife in our contemporary world of war, injustice and greed.

Concluding Prayer

Great and generous God of justice and hope,
before you my life is transparent.
Banish from my heart all resistance and false pride.
Teach me to challenge injustice with courage and
    patience,
and to refrain from acting purely out of anger.
Trusting in your gentle compassion,
flood me with your peace.
Fill me with silence and stillness
so that I may hear you inviting me
to surrender my life in love to you.
I make this prayer in the name of Jesus,
my friend, companion, and soul guide. Amen.

PSALM 39   *Struggling with Anger*

I resolved, 'I will keep watch over my steps,
lest I sin with my tongue.
I will keep a muzzle on my mouth,
as long as a wicked person is near me.'

I was silent, still, speechless, but to no avail.
My distress increased, my heart smouldered within me.
While I mused, the fire blazed up.
Then I broke into speech:

'Lord, let me know my end,
and what the measure of my days is,

that I may know how frail I am.
You have given my days a very short span,
and my lifetime is as nothing in your sight.'

No one endures any longer than a breath.
Indeed all walk about as mere shadows.
Mere futility their hustle and bustle,
heaping up provisions without knowing for whom.

So now, Lord, what do I wait for?
My only hope is in you.
Save me from all my sins,
do not make me the taunt of fools.

Hear my prayer, O Lord,
and pay heed to my cry.
Do not be silent at my tears!
For I am your migrant,
a nomad like all my ancestors.

NOTES ON PSALM 39

I will keep … I will keep: The poet's resolve is strengthened through using the same verb twice in these opening lines, as if to emphasise his commitment to be really careful in what he says in tricky situations.

a muzzle: This unusual word occurs only here as a noun in the Hebrew Bible, but the verb occurs also, in the sense of muzzling an ox (Deuteronomy 25:4), or damming a pond (Sirach 48:17), or blocking the way of travellers (Ezekiel 39:11). The image is very effective, not unlike the modern expression of zipping one's lips, lest inappropriate speech should emerge.

near me: The implication here is that of impending confrontation by a person of evil intent.

silent, still, speechless: The poet uses three different verbs to convey how focused his effort was to keep his mouth muzzled.

distress increased: The strain was too great, hence the inner turmoil.

my heart smoldered: The image of inner turmoil and distress now changes into that of a heart on fire, ready to blaze into an unstoppable conflagration.

I broke into speech: The pot boils over, the coiled spring snaps, the house of cards collapses, and one's resolve evaporates into thin air.

'Lord, let me know my end': Instead of addressing the enemy in the heat of the moment, as one might have expected, the poet now turns to God, with some very deep requests.

how frail I am: The fragile nature of human existence is at stake here. It is conveyed by a word which elsewhere in the Bible is used of life ceasing, or of green shoots failing to appear.

a very short span: The poet uses a rare word here which reinforces the transitory and fleeting nature of life: 'a mere handbreadth'.

a breath: A very effective measure of the shortness of one's life, this image is further enhanced by the notion of humans 'walking about as mere shadows', accumulating wealth 'without knowing for whom'.

My only hope is in you: Against this background of uncertainty, the poet turns to God as the only wellspring from which he can draw strength and focus.

pay heed to my cry: The psalm ends with a plea that God would be moved by the poet's distress and tears.

your migrant: A resident alien, or someone without full civic documentation.

a nomad: This word also evokes the transient nature of one's journey through life.

Suggestions for Praying with Psalm 39

Have you ever been in a situation where you know you should keep your thoughts to yourself lest you lose control of your tongue? If this happens to you from time to time, then you can take some consolation from Psalm 39. The psalm author begins with a confident assertion of self-control: 'I resolved…'. His pledge to watch what he says and to muzzle his mouth may sound familiar. However, the tone soon changes as anger grows within, and the resolution falls apart: 'I was silent, still, speechless, but to no avail … my heart smouldered within me … and I broke into speech'. Does the experience underlying this powerful description sound familiar? And if so, what can you do about it?

Here again, the psalm can help, for the poet then becomes more reflective. Instead of letting fly at his adversary, whom he rightly or wrongly sees as the source of his distress, he turns to God. As he mulls over the transient nature of life, he comes to see the futility of getting too hot under the collar over minor issues. This psalm can be of help when you need to draw back a little from a heated argument or dispute, and gain some space in which to evaluate what is happening. Viewed from a distance, it may be that you might even be able to laugh at yourself. And, in spite of tears and feelings of foolishness, following in the psalmist's footsteps, you can be helped to remember that life is fleeting, and that your deepest hopes rest in God.

Concluding Prayer

Almighty and ever-faithful God
companion of my life's journey,
when I get drawn into conflict
or lose my temper for whatever reason,
alert me to your grace-filled presence.
Grant me your strength to be patient.
Leaving my fears and anxieties behind,
help me to stand back and be still.
In these moments of silence, work on my inmost being,

so that I may be open to you, my only hope,
the source and final purpose of my life.
This prayer I make in Jesus' name. Amen.

4 Why Me?

Psalms of Puzzlement

It is striking how we instinctively search for joy and steer clear of suffering. Joy gives us respite on the long road of life and an appreciation of tremendous beauty in the midst of the mundane. Yet, suffering is a natural part of life with much to teach us. It's a paradox that suffering and joy come from the same place: they are the finger of God beckoning us to grow beyond where we are now so that new and wonderful things can happen to us again. And, in all of this, the psalms can really help.

The great majority of psalms witness to the experience of suffering. Only a few manage to escape some echo of it. Suffering takes many shades, and in this the psalms mirror our lives. Allowing us a 2,500-year-old snapshot of the human condition, they assure us that our hopes and fears are not unlike those of ancient times. In our lives we experience many moods. Sometimes we feel good, other times wretched and in panic. In times of anxiety, pain and distress, like the psalmist, we ask 'Why?' And often we do not find an immediate answer.

Suffering is perhaps one of the very few things in life that can only be appreciated once it is over. To seek suffering for its own sake is neither normal nor healthy. Yet without some experience of suffering we could ask whether we would ever come to know God very personally. If we had everything we need would we really make space for God? Suffering of some kind seems to be the only thing strong enough to destabilise our egotism and our ignorance. Healthy religion shows us what to do with our pain and with what seems unfair or tragic in our lives. If we do not learn to transform our pain we will surely transmit it. The great mystery about Jesus' life is that, while he tried to alleviate suffering wherever he encountered it, he himself was not spared, but through love endured suffering unto death on a cross.

The psalms often begin on a low note and describe the inner turmoil of the author. Then a turning point is reached where suffering is somehow tolerated, after which comes a measure of acceptance, and finally even joy and thanksgiving. The American theologian Walter Brueggemann has described this movement from sorrow to joy in the psalms as the journey from 'pit' to 'wing'. Many psalms contain this movement from asking 'Why?' to voicing expressions of trust. The biblical metaphors of 'pit' and 'wing' are very powerful. Like the modern poem about footprints in the sand, they articulate the conviction that God has been with the speaker through the darkest moments. The image of 'pit' describes the fear of abandonment, whether in this life, or after death. It can be helpful also to remember that in Old Testament times belief in the afterlife had not yet been clearly formulated.

If the image of pit symbolises abandonment, that of 'wing' stands for God's protection. Taking refuge under God's wings is a homely image, as we imagine the divine Protector like a mother hen sheltering her chicks under her wing. This is also a very feminine image of God – a nice counterbalance to the mainly masculine images of God in the Bible. The psalmist, no less than ourselves, would be well aware that God has no wings – or hands either for that matter – but it is a wonderfully protective image in the midst of turmoil. Psalm 57:1 states confidently that 'in the shadow of your wings I will take refuge till the destroying storms pass by', while Psalm 63:7 celebrates that 'you have been my help, and in the shadow of your wings I sing for joy.'

Psalm 30   *Rescued from the Abyss*

I will praise you, Lord, for you have drawn me up,
and have not let my enemies rejoice over me.
Lord, you have lifted me up out of Sheol,
you have preserved me from going down to the Pit.

O you faithful of the Lord, sing to him.
Give thanks in recalling his holiness.
One may lie down weeping at nightfall,
but cries of joy come with the morning.

To you, Lord, I cry out.
With the Lord I plead for mercy:
'What gain is there from my death,
from my going down to the abyss?
Can dust give you thanks,
or proclaim your faithfulness?'

You have turned my mourning into dancing.
You have taken off my sackcloth and clothed me with
    joy.
So my whole being will sing unceasingly to you, Lord.
My God, forever will I give you thanks.

NOTES ON PSALM 30

you have drawn me up: The poet begins on a note of praise because he
    has experienced the joy of release from a threatening situation. The
    imagery underlying his choice of verb (to draw up out of) prepares the
    way for the last two lines of this first stanza which speak explicitly of
    Sheol and Pit, both images of being down in the depths.

lifted me up ... preserved me: Both verbs evoke the sense of relief on being rescued from something awful.

Sheol: The terms Sheol and Pit are used interchangeably to describe a shadowy grey place of sojourn without hope. This Old Testament imagery must not be equated with the much later-developed concept of hell as a place of fiery punishment.

you faithful of the Lord: The speaker enthusiastically invites the wider group of worshippers to join with him in celebrating his release from anguish, and possibly even from death.

Give thanks: God is to be thanked, not just because the poet is overjoyed at having being rescued from the abyss, but especially because God is all holy.

weeping at nightfall: The poet's contrast of the natural tendency to be weighed down at nightfall with renewed energy at the dawning of a new day is perhaps an image of the situation before and after rescue from the Pit.

I cry out: The psalmist returns to the theme of imploring God's help and mercy in a time of great need, and imminent death.

What gain is there from my death?: The reasoning behind this question reflects the prevailing views of the psalmist's time. Since death was perceived as the end, after which there was nothing further to do except decompose in the darkness of Sheol or the Pit, the psalmist argues with God that it would be much better that he be preserved from death so that he could then continue to thank and praise God.

turned my mourning into dancing: This last stanza is full of the poet's exuberance and delight at being rescued from imminent danger. His spontaneous response is to thank God with his whole being.

Suggestions for Praying with Psalm 30

The journey in this psalm can be adapted to many modern situations, and provides an excellent illustration of the paradox of moving from suffering to joy, from despair to courage, from pit to wing. Can you recall a situation in which you were close to death, either factually or symbolically? It may have been a doctor's diagnosis, or a near escape from a road accident? Or perhaps it was a situation of being cut off from family or friends? And then something occurred so that the 'death-sentence' was lifted. It might be helpful to use this psalm as a way of journeying through the experience, so that you can reach a point of thanking God for his personal care of your every moment. As the poet muses over the futility of giving in when feelings of depression and hopelessness overwhelm, perhaps you too can be helped to reach a point of trust, in spite of overwhelming odds. Take each stanza and enter into its imagery and mood, lingering on whatever appeals to you. Allow it to express your desire to surrender to God's providence. Allow it to deepen your appreciation of how often he draws you up out of the abyss.

Concluding Prayer

Great caring God,
you are faithful beyond my imagining.
Draw me up out of the deep hole of my fears and
    anxieties
so that I may acknowledge the holiness of your being.
Lift me out of the pit of self-pity
so that I may notice your loving providence
in every detail of my life.
When I fall down into the abyss of grief,
turn my mourning into dancing,
and let my whole being sing unceasingly of your love.
I make this prayer in the name of Jesus,
who sets me free and gives me new life. Amen.

PSALM 16   *Not abandoned to the Pit*

Keep me safe, O God,
for in you I seek refuge.
I say to the Lord, 'You are my Lord.
Apart from you I have no good.'

I bless the Lord who guides me,
even at night my heart exhorts me.
I keep the Lord before me always,
for with him at my right hand, nothing can shake me.

Therefore my heart rejoices, and my whole being exults,
my body also rests secure.
For you will not abandon me to Sheol,
or let your faithful one see the Pit.

You will teach me the path of life,
the fullness of joy in your presence,
at your right hand delight for ever.

NOTES ON PSALM 16

Keep me safe: This psalm opens, as do many petition psalms, with a plea
for some kind of protection or rescue from distress.

Apart from you I have no good: The opening plea is followed by an affirmation of faith in the Lord and a declaration of total trust.

I bless the Lord: To 'bless' the Lord is another way of offering praise and
thanks to the Lord.

who guides me: This guidance is a general term which includes teaching,
counselling, and advising, as well as providential events leading to new
insights.

I keep the Lord always before me: This sense of continual awareness of
God's presence in the life of the psalmist was applied to Jesus by the early
Christians (Acts 2:25). For them, and for us, Jesus is the one who is most
intimately and ever present to God.

at my right hand: In the Bible the 'right hand' is a symbol of power and
authority. It is also a symbol of honour, which is the case here. Thus, the
psalmist is confident that, with God at his right hand, he cannot but be
totally secure.

Therefore my heart rejoices: This sense of God's powerful presence is a
source of joy and delight for the psalmist.

My body also rests secure: His sense of trust in God's protection includes
his physical body.

For you will not abandon me to Sheol: The real source of the psalmist's
confidence lies in his trust that God will protect him in the here and
now, and not let him face immediate death.

your faithful one see the Pit: The early Greek version of the Bible
translated 'pit' here as 'corruption'. The content of this verse became
particularly important to the early Christian community, because, reading their Scriptures in Greek, they interpreted this line as referring to
Jesus. They understood it as a prophecy of his resurrection and immor-
tality: Jesus did 'not see corruption' (Acts 2:27, 31; 13:35). We too can
pray 'not to experience corruption' in any of its modern forms.

teach me the path of life: This is a typical wisdom metaphor, concerned
with an upright manner of walking the path of life so that it leads to
God. Walking the path of life is the theme statement for the entire book
of Psalms, as clearly set forth in the opening lines of Psalm 1. This first
psalm speaks of a moral choice of following the way of good or the way
of evil, offering our human freedom the option of adhering to God's will
as expressed in the goodness of creation, and in God's self-disclosure to
humanity.

The fullness of joy in your presence: This joy will be the fruit of faithful adherence to God's will during our lifetime. The early Christians

applied this verse to Jesus, who was the one who experienced this joy in God's presence in the fullest possible way (Acts 2:28).

Suggestions for Praying with Psalm 16

This psalm is a wonderful celebration of awareness of God's presence in our life, and a celebration of the power of this presence. With God at our right hand, nothing can shake us. Day and night this amazing presence is there to guide and prompt us. God's enduring presence is the source of deep inner peace and happiness, and a guarantee of walking the path of life into eternity. God is always present, incarnate in every moment, and present to those who know how to tune into this presence.

You don't have to be in a certain place, you don't have to be a perfect person to experience this wonderful presence. God cannot be less present in one situation or more present in another. God is fully present everywhere and always. It is we who are often absent.

Like the early Christian community, we can also understand this psalm as fulfilled in Jesus in every aspect of his life, death and resurrection. We can pray this psalm in gratitude for the hope it gives us. We can ask for a deeper awareness of God's loving presence. We can also pray this psalm with our loved ones in mind, our family and friends who have already walked the path of life in God's love and who now enjoy the fullness of joy in God's presence.

Concluding Prayer

All-embracing and ever-present God,
when the storms of life threaten to overwhelm me,
clasp my hand tightly and keep me safe.
May I grow ever more mindful of your loving presence,
so that nothing can shake my trust in you.

With Jesus, your faithful one,
bring me safely home to unbounded joy in your
    presence.
This prayer I make to you, O God ever present. Amen.

PSALM 61   *From Pit to Wing*

Hear my cry, O God,
give heed to my prayer!
From the end of the earth I call,
as my heart grows faint.

You lead me to a rock
that is high above me.
For you are my refuge,
a tower of strength against the foe.

Oh that I might dwell forever in your tent,
take refuge under the shelter of your wings.
Then I will sing praises to your name forever,
as I fulfill my vows day after day.

NOTES ON PSALM 61

Hear my cry: This psalm opens with a typical plea for help. Its second line
    rephrases and expands this cry for help, using a verb which asks God to
    listen carefully to the poet's prayer.

From the end of the earth: The speaker's request seems to be made from a
    psychological distance, which feels as though it were actually from 'the
    end of the earth'.

as my heart grows faint: Such is his distress that the poet becomes
    progressively more faint-hearted, and in need of help.

a rock: In the psalms God is often compared to a rock, symbol of solidity and security, durability and constancy. To be 'led up to a rock' implies the metaphor of being rescued or brought up from the Pit, or from Sheol to a place of great safety.

my refuge: A refuge or tower was a defensive structure in ancient times that was essential in times of war. That it should be strong and reliable goes without saying. The psalmist describes God as metaphorically providing the necessary strong and reliable shelter. The biblical phrase 'a tower of strength' has passed into everyday language.

dwell forever in your tent: God's tent, often called 'the tent of meeting' was a very powerful symbol of God's presence. The psalmist desires to dwell continually in this sacred space of encounter and protection.

shelter of your wings: This image occurs in a number of psalms, and contrasts with that of 'pit'. Whereas 'pit' evokes images of danger and peril, that of God's 'wing' speaks of sanctuary, tenderness and nurture.

sing praises: The word psalm or 'song of praise' comes from the Hebrew verb used here.

to your name: God's name is what the biblical writers use when they want to speak of God's very being, of God's majesty and mystery. In today's language we would speak of singing praise to the very person of God.

fulfill my vows: Typical petition psalms include a promise to do something in thanksgiving for having had one's prayer answered. Sometimes this meant the offering of a sacrifice in the temple. Or it could mean the singing of hymns or songs of praise, as in this case.

Suggestions for Praying with Psalm 61

In this psalm there is a clear movement 'from pit to wing'. In the opening lines the poet begs God to listen to his cry for help, which is made as though 'from the end of the earth'. This place of abandonment could be described as 'the depths of the pit'. It is a place where a person understandably feels faint-hearted. Then, as the psalm unfolds, the author gradually comes to recognise God as a tower of strength

– a rock with all its character of solidity and reliability. The psalm contains a journey, beginning with a cry for help in the opening lines. This journey reaches completion as the poet acknowledges his desire to remain forever safe in God's presence, secure in the shelter of the divine 'wings'. This is a deceptively short psalm, but it covers a long and often painful journey in real time.

To pray with this psalm you might first try to stay with each phrase of the opening verse. Allow yourself to enter more fully into how it connects with your own experience, particularly that of suffering or of bereavement. Then, as you become more accepting of the situation that is causing you to be fainthearted, you may be able to enter more fully into the mood of the last lines, and pray for the grace of trust and surrender that it so beautifully expresses.

Concluding Prayer

Merciful, caring and nourishing God,
you are my enduring rock of stability,
and my tower of strength in danger.
Be with me as I cry to you in my pain.
Listen to my heart's hunger.
Place me under the shelter of your wings,
that I may live securely in your presence.
This prayer I make in Jesus' name. Amen.

PSALM 17   *Secure under God's Wings*

Hear a just cause, O Lord!
Attend to my cry.
Pay heed to my prayer
from lips free of fraud.

From you comes my vindication,
your eyes see what is right.
You have tested my heart,
searched it in the night.

My steps have kept to your paths,
my feet have not slipped.
I call upon you, for you answer me, O God.
Incline your ear to me, hear what I say.

Show me your wonderful love,
you who save with your right arm.
Keep me as the apple of the eye,
hide me in the shadow of your wings.

NOTES ON PSALM 17

a just cause: The psalmist begins by turning to God as judge, to the only One who will hear his case without bias.

Attend to my cry: The typical invocation of petition psalms now follows.

lips free of fraud: The psalmist reminds God again of his integrity.

my vindication: The poet continues with the certainty that he will receive just judgement from God, who is unprejudiced and sees things as they truly are.

tested my heart: Confidence comes from knowing that God can see the author's true motives, and therefore he has nothing to fear.

in the night: From the biblical perspective night time is when people think that they can get away with things. But the poet is happy to have all his actions — even those done under the cover of darkness — submitted to God's examination.

have kept to your paths: He restates the integrity of his moral life, this time using the imagery of walking along the right path, from which his feet have not strayed.

for you answer me: The psalmist's confidence springs from the certainty that God is One who continues to answer his pleadings (the verb is in a continuous present tense).

Incline your ear: The metaphor here is that of God bending down to listen. The imagery evokes the confidence of small children who know from experience that their parents bend down to listen not only to what they are saying, but also to what they are not yet able to put into words.

Show me your wonderful love: The poet begs for some sign of God's faithful love, to demonstrate that God is really listening.

with your right arm: This image of God's saving power is often used in the Psalms, and elsewhere in the Bible.

the apple of the eye: Attested even earlier than the King James Bible (1611), and also found in Shakespeare (1564-1616), this expression has found its way into popular speech in English. It's a graphic way of expressing how a person or thing is very precious to another person. In its original biblical form, this idiom literally means 'little man' of the eye, a diminutive form of 'man'. This is a reference to the tiny reflection of yourself that you can see in other people's eyes when you look into them closely. In using this daring idiom the psalmist is asking to remain in a very special relationship to his God, to be kept as safely as one would guard the pupil of one's own eye from danger.

Hide me: The more usual biblical verb for this idiom is 'to find refuge' or 'shelter'.

the shadow of your wings: The psalmist looks for a safe haven, concealed beneath the shadow or protective shade of God's wings.

Suggestions for Praying with Psalm 17

The mood of this psalm is one of confidence in God. This sense of trust is expressed in each stanza, using different images. In the first stanza, the poet presents his petition in judicial terms, asking God to hear his case, which is made with 'lips free of fraud'. In the second stanza the poet expands on his petition, but this time with the focus on God as the one who will vindicate, the one who sees, tests and searches the inner motivations of the petitioner. Then the focus shifts back on the psalmist, on his steps and his feet, as they walk along the way of God. Because of his sincerity and integrity, the psalmist feels secure in repeating his petition, and that God will bend down to listen. The final stanza contains two further beautiful images of trust and intimacy which sum up the movement of the psalm as a whole: the poet asks to be protected by God as the apple of the eye, and to be sheltered under the divine wings.

This psalm can be helpful for prayer in almost any situation. If you feel confident in God's love, then its various lines can simply be repeated gently, as you rest in trusting relationship, and ask for the gift of growing in faith, hope and love. On the other hand, if you are anxious and undergoing a period of distress, this psalm may help you to cope with doubt and worry, as you seek reassurance and courage.

Concluding Prayer

Wonderful God of justice and hope,
bend down to hear my plea for help.
Before you my life is transparent,
guide my steps along your paths.
You reveal yourself in ways great and small,
as you show me your wonderful love.
When the harsh winds of adversity howl about me,
hide me in the shelter of your wings.
Great lover of my soul, protect and nourish me,
and keep me as the apple of your eye.
I make this prayer in the name of the triune God. Amen

5 I'm Sorry!

Psalms of Repentance

The Gospels tell us that many sick and troubled people approached Jesus using the simple plea, 'Lord, have mercy!' This attitude in prayer is deeply scriptural. The Greek words *Kyrie eleison* in the penitential rite at Mass might suggest that this formula has to do only with begging for forgiveness of sins. But closer examination of the psalms shows that this plea, while often linked with a sense of one's sinfulness, is considerably wider than seeking forgiveness of sins.

God's mercy includes tenderness and compassion, covenant faithfulness, faithful love, and uprightness. The word for mercy in Hebrew comes from a stem meaning 'womb', thus providing us with a powerful maternal image of God's compassion. When we plead 'Lord, have mercy' or *Kyrie eleison* we are begging first and foremost that God take pity on us, that he show us his faithful love. In more specific circumstances, we may also be asking for his forgiveness.

Forgiveness in the Bible is predominantly a divine action whereby God takes away the barriers which separate us from his presence, thereby opening up the way to reconciliation and the restoration of friendship. Thus, forgiveness expresses a religious relationship between God and human beings. It can also refer to forgiveness by one person of another, an aspect which was especially prominent in the teaching of Jesus, and is enshrined in the Our Father.

Various metaphors are used in Hebrew to express forgiveness. That of 'taking away' occurs most frequently, while that of 'making amends' is linked with atonement. Other images include 'blotting out' and 'wiping away'. Human beings cannot live without God, and only the removal of sin can enable us to have a life of integrity and wholeness. But Israel's God is merciful, and has no pleasure in the death of a sinner. Through the covenant this compassionate God offers mercy to his people, so that in spite of human backsliding and unfaithfulness the covenant continues to mediate the mercy and faithfulness of God. This is because this mercy is based, not on human achievements, but upon the holiness and reliability of God.

Since the sixth century AD, seven psalms (6, 32, 38, 51, 103, 130, 143) have come to be known in the Christian tradition as 'penitential psalms'. The most famous of this group of psalms is Psalm 51, often called the *Miserere* (its first word in Latin). This psalm is a particularly beautiful one, and illustrates well the link between God's compassion and God's forgiveness contained in the cry, 'Lord, have mercy!' We will explore it in two parts.

PSALM 51 (I)   *A Compassionate and Forgiving God*

Have pity on me, O God,
in your faithful love.
In your abundant compassion
wipe away my offences.

Wash me thoroughly from my guilt,
from my sin cleanse me.
For my offences I know,
my sin is ever before me.

Against you, you alone, have I sinned,
what is evil in your sight I have done,

so you are just in your sentence
and blameless in your judgement.

Indeed, I was born guilty,
sinful from the moment my mother conceived me.
Because you delight in inner truth,
teach me wisdom in my inmost being.

NOTES ON PSALM 51 (I)

Have pity on me: Although the opening petition of this psalm is tradi-
tionally translated as 'Have mercy on me' (*miserere mei* in Latin), in
its original form the verb used actually means 'to have pity on', 'to feel
sympathy for', and 'to be gracious to'.

in your faithful love: God's faithful love is central to his covenantal relationship with his people. It is steadfast, enduring, and always loyal. It is
a forgiving love.

abundant compassion: At the heart of God's unstinted compassion lies
the powerful imagery of the maternal womb. As a mother cannot forget
the child of her womb, so God's abundant maternal love can never be
annulled.

wipe away: This is the first of a number of 'cleansing' images central to
this psalm.

my offences: There is a rich biblical vocabulary relating to the concept
of sin. An offence or 'rebellious act' is one such key word, and is used
principally to denote infidelity or a rebellious attitude to the covenant
obligations. Here the psalmist asks God to cancel out his personal failure to be loyal to the covenant.

my guilt: The Hebrew word here implies a twisted or distorted condition, and describes someone who is crooked or morally deformed. In
the vocabulary of sin, it is usually rendered as 'guilt', suggesting some
ongoing negative impact on the person.

my sin: This is the most common word in the Bible relating to the concept of sin. It means 'missing the mark'. One who 'sins' fails to meet what is expected in relation to God, and by extension, to another person.

my offences I know: This psalm is striking for its honesty and willingness to admit and confront personal failure. Its author does not hide behind conventional shady behaviours, but admits personal responsibility.

Against you, you alone: Also striking is the poet's awareness of how personal sin impacts on one's relationship with God.

evil in your sight: The psalmist is only too aware of having done evil, and accepts that God's judgements in this regard are upright.

born guilty: The author intensifies his awareness of sinfulness by pushing it back to his conception and birth. He is not speaking of 'original sin' (a theological concept developed by St Augustine in the fifth century AD), but with poetic licence is emphasizing his acute realization of being a thoroughly sinful creature.

my mother conceived me: In parallelism with the previous line, here too there is no sense of having been conceived through an inappropriate sexual relationship on the part of the speaker's mother. Rather, in graphic terms he is seeking to convey awareness of being a sinner from the very moment his personal existence began.

Because you delight in inner truth: Although painfully conscious of his sinful condition, the psalmist courageously acknowledges that the only way forward is to trust that God is on his side, and wants him to be upright and truthful in his personal life.

teach me wisdom: God is the source of all truth, good living, and wisdom.

Suggestions for Praying with Psalm 51 (1)

The author of this psalm is painfully conscious of being a sinful creature through and through. He repeatedly asks God to wash, cleanse, and wipe away all traces of sin, offence, evil, and guilt. He explicitly acknowledges that he is responsible for his sinful actions. In the Christian tradition this psalm has been consistently linked with penitence. A favourite within the Irish monastic tradition, it is frequently used in contemporary reconciliation services.

Praying meditatively through each line of this psalm can help us contemporary Christians acknowledge specific failings and offences against family members and our wider circle of friends, acquaintances and colleagues. It can also help us tap into the fragility of our own relationship with God, and of how easily we can drift away and be left without adequate nourishment and support in meeting the challenges of life today. It can also help us to tap into our sense of sinfulness on a broader canvas, and acknowledge that we are part of a sinful society, often reinforcing various patterns of oppression and dishonesty through inaction.

Even if the focus in this psalm appears to be on sin and sinfulness, there is nevertheless a very positive note throughout. God is gracious, compassionate, faithful, and just. God is also one who teaches wisdom to those whose hearts are open to learn. It would be important to balance a sense of personal frailty with these strong and confident notes that the psalmist sounds throughout the psalm.

Concluding Prayer

God of abundant compassion and understanding,
you who are faithful beyond my wildest dreams
and more loving that I can ever deserve,
flood my being with your healing power
and restore me to wholeness in your cleansing grace.
Although I have often failed to follow your will,
and have sinned against you, time and again,
with your help I desire to begin afresh.
This I pray in the name of Jesus, your Son and my
    Saviour. Amen.

PSALM 51 (II) *A New and Unwavering Spirit*

Cleanse me with hyssop till I am clean.
Wash me till I am whiter than snow.
Hide your face from my sins,
and wipe away all my iniquities.

A clean heart create in me, O God,
renew within me an unwavering spirit.
Do not banish me from your presence,
or take your holy spirit away from me.

Let me again rejoice in your deliverance,
may a generous spirit sustain me.
Lord, open my lips,
that my mouth may proclaim your praise.

You have no delight in sacrifice,
if I were to bring a burnt offering, you would
        not accept it.
True sacrifice to God is a contrite spirit,
a contrite and humbled heart, O God, you will
        not spurn.

NOTES ON PSALM 51 (II)

hyssop: A plant of uncertain identity, the Israelites used hyssop to sprinkle
    water in purification rituals. They also used it to apply blood onto their
    doorposts during Passover.
Hide your face: The hiding of God's face is positive here, a sign of grace
    and forgiveness, and not of divine displeasure, as elsewhere in the Bible.

A clean heart: Often translated as 'a pure heart', the usual context is that of ritual purity. But this psalm goes far beyond the merely ritual to include the ethical dimensions of human behaviour.

renew: The appeal here evokes the 'new heart and new spirit' of Ezekiel 18:31 and 36:26, with its focus on ethical renewal.

an unwavering spirit: The adjective comes from a Hebrew word for solidity, firmness of foundation. It is often translated as 'steadfast'.

banish: The verb here is quite strong: 'cast away, drive out'.

your holy spirit: In the Old Testament God's spirit was synonymous with God himself, with a focus here on God's holiness. At the psalmist's time it would not have had any further symbolism. It is understandable however that the early Christian believers interpreted this phrase as foreshadowing the Holy Spirit, and hence the trinitarian nature of God. This sense of searching the Scriptures for their fuller meaning permits us today to do likewise, without bypassing the original context.

sustain me: Parallel to rejoicing in the experience of God's saving love, the poet asks that he be supported by a strong motivating energy.

You have no delight in sacrifice: Side by side with the elaborate Old Testament sacrificial structure, there was also an underlying awareness that this structure was meaningless if not the expression of authentic moral values.

True sacrifice: The biblical prophets were adamant that worship involving animal sacrifice was meaningful only if it expressed authentic moral values. The psalmist is expressing a conviction that was to reach its climax in John 4:23-24, which speaks of 'worshippers in spirit and in truth'.

Suggestions for Praying with Psalm 51 (II)

In this second part of Psalm 51 the poet repeats his request for forgiveness, using again the imagery of purification and washing. The note of joy and gratitude is strong, and invites us modern readers to recall the joy we experience when we receive forgiveness from someone we have hurt. But above all, it is the experience of God's forgiveness that is the main source of joy in this psalm — a gift we can celebrate as enthusiastically as the psalm's author: 'Lord, open my lips, that my mouth may declare your praise.' The words of John Newton's 'Amazing Grace' are a modern expression of this sense of liberation that forgiveness can bring about. Allow the various images and desires of the psalm to connect with your own faith journey.

Concluding Prayer

Generous God of healing and forgiveness,
breathe your Holy Spirit anew on my fragile being.
Renew my deep desire for wholeness and integrity.
Purify me and draw me into your creative energy
so that I may rejoice in your saving love.
Accept my contrite heart, O Lord, and lift my spirit,
until my awakened self can rejoice and sing your praise.
In the name of the triune God I make this prayer. Amen.

PSALM 103 *A Merciful and Gracious God*

Bless the Lord, O my soul,
and let all my being bless his holy name.
Bless the Lord, O my soul,
and forget none of his benefits –

who forgives all your guilt,
who heals all your diseases,
who refreshes your vitality with what is good,
your youth is renewed like the eagle's.

The Lord is tender and compassionate,
long-suffering and rich in faithful love.
He does not treat us according to our sins,
nor repay us as befits our iniquities.

For as the heavens tower over the earth,
so strong is his faithful love towards those who fear
    him;
as far as east is from west,
so far from us does he put our offences.

As tenderly as a father treats his children,
so the Lord treats those who fear him.
For he knows how we are formed,
he is mindful that we are but dust.

The Lord's faithful love
is from eternity and forever
on those who fear him.
Bless the Lord, O my soul.

NOTES ON PSALM 103

Bless: The primary meaning of the Hebrew verb *barak* is 'to bend the
knees', but it is most often used in its applied sense of 'to worship, praise,
bless'. Here, the psalmist encourages himself to bless God.

O my soul: In the Old Testament 'soul' never means the immortal soul,
as it does in Greek thinking. Rather it expresses the life principle or the
living being, but always as appearing in some fleshly form, without
which it would not exist. It refers to the self as representing the totality
of feeling, and is often, as here, a more emotionally charged alternative
for a personal pronoun.

all my being: This phrase refers to the innermost depths of a person, and echoes the first line, with its reference to 'my soul' as emphasizing the individual who is speaking.

his holy name: God's name was the equivalent of God's selfhood, and central to God's identity is his essential holiness or mysterious otherness.

guilt ... diseases: Both moral and bodily ailments are taken care of by this loving God.

vitality: The most probable meaning of the obscure Hebrew word here has to do with one's vital energy.

renewed like the eagle: For the biblical writers, the eagle was a symbol of speed. It was also prized for its lofty grandeur, its gentle and protective care for its young, and its youthful vigour as here. A similar image occurs at Isaiah 40:31: 'Those who trust in the Lord will renew their strength, they will soar as with eagles' wings'.

tender and compassionate: These two qualities portray a God who cares beyond reckoning. The first quality is linked with the Hebrew word for the womb.

those who fear him: This phrase occurs three times in this psalm. It evokes not a cringing fear before a terrifying deity, but an attitude of awe before the mystery of a loving God, an attitude born out of gratitude for God's unmerited love.

tenderly: This adverb is also linked to the Hebrew word for the womb.

how we are formed ... we are but dust: These two lines allude to the Genesis 2:7 narrative depicting how the Lord God formed human beings out of the dust of the ground.

Bless the Lord, O my soul: The psalm ends as it began, with an exhortation to bless God for his generous and forgiving love.

Suggestions for Praying with Psalm 103

The mood in this psalm is upbeat. Its author knows that he is in need of healing from both sin and bodily infirmity. But the dominant note is one of praise and gratitude for blessings received. There is an intimacy too, for the psalmist's God is one who tenderly bends down to support his children in their difficulties. There is energy in the image of the poet's youth being revitalised like that of the proverbial eagle. The metaphors here convey a vitality that moves beyond actual youth to hint at the new life that flows at any age from the healing touch of a compassionate God.

This is a psalm to savour as it contains many strong and positive images of a God who bends down, and a psalmist who is confident of being loved and cared for. Allow its richness to flow over you through reading and rereading it slowly. Then it can be helpful to stay with one or other of its images, with what becomes attractive to you, and meets you in your particular situation.

Concluding Prayer

Almighty, forgiving, and most intimate God,
barefoot and with bowed head I come before you.
I know I need your healing in both body and spirit.
But I also know that you are full of tenderness and pity,
and that you place my failings as far as east is from west.
Lift me up to know your faithful love in my life.
Remind me that you are my Father,
the One who formed me, and knows me through and
    through.
Within the loving and healing arms of God,
I make this prayer. Amen.

PSALM 130 *Out of the Depths*

From the depths I call to you, O Lord.
Lord, hear my cry!

Let your ears listen attentively
to the cry of my pleadings!

If you, O Lord, should keep account of iniquities,
Lord, who could stand?
But with you is forgiveness,
and so you are held in awe.

I wait for the Lord, my soul waits,
and for his word I hope.
My soul yearns for the Lord
more than those longing for dawn,
than those longing for dawn.

Let Israel hope in the Lord!
For with the Lord is faithful love,
and with him is full redemption.
It is he who will redeem Israel from all its iniquities.

NOTES ON PSALM 130

From the depths: The Hebrew word evokes a deep ravine or deep water, and the use of the plural in this metaphor emphasises the most remote depths in which the psalmist feels he is drowning.

hear my cry: Because the poet has sunk so low, he imagines he has to raise his voice as loudly as possible to attract divine attention.

attentively: Aware that, in his deep distress, his pleas may be incoherent, the psalmist begs God to listen carefully.

my pleadings: The plural implies repeated entreaties.

keep account of iniquities: The image is a negative one, which the poet rejects as incompatible with his experience of God.

who could stand: Who could endure a situation in which an unforgiving God would keep account of wrongdoing? A scenario of this kind would be unthinkable to the psalmist.

forgiveness: The poet is convinced that the possibility of forgiveness lies in the hands of God alone.

held in awe: Divine pardon means that the barriers separating the sinner from God are removed, and the penitent has a new awareness of God, expressed in an attitude of awe.

I wait: Waiting for God is an action that comes from within the person, an attitude of patient attentiveness that is repeated in this line.

I hope: By contrast, the action of hoping has its focus outside the person. It is an action centred on God's word as the object of hope. This action of hoping is picked up again in the last stanza.

longing for dawn: The sun's rising is guaranteed by the unfailing laws of nature. The psalmist uses a powerful image of the longing for dawn of those keeping a night watch. His yearning for God is much stronger than theirs for dawn. He is confident that his dark night of distress will give way to the warm sun of God's faithful love. The repetition of the longing for dawn in the last line of the third stanza serves to underscore the contrast between the natural longing for morning of ordinary night-shift workers and the longing for God of the person crying 'from the depths'.

Israel: In the last stanza the poet moves from the individual to the nation, Israel, which is mentioned twice in these closing lines. This movement illustrates how some psalms developed from being individual compositions to their being adopted for communal use in worship.

full redemption: God is not restricted by human obstacles. His redeeming love knows no limitations, and overcomes human frailty.

Suggestions for Praying with Psalm 130

Waiting is an inescapable fact of life. What is the quality of your waiting? For a bus, for a phone call, for a visitor, for a job? And especially how do you wait when in distress, pain, or darkness? Although this psalm begins with a cry 'from the depths', it is essentially a psalm of trustful waiting, of waiting with hope. It was probably included among the traditional penitential psalms because of its second stanza. This confidently expresses the conviction that God is not a divine accountant keeping exact records of our sins in his ledger.

There are times in our lives when God seems particularly absent, and our cry really comes 'from the depths'. This psalm can give us courage to trust that God's coming 'is as certain as the dawn' (Hosea 6:3). It does not require much effort to bring to mind how the movement of this psalm can help in your experience of searching for meaning in distress. Allow the lines to connect with your need for hope, and for encouragement to wait through the dark night till the warmth of God's faithful love can reach you, and eventually help you to cope with your doubts and anxieties.

This psalm is often used as part of funeral liturgies. In the midst of the pain of loss and bereavement, it can be helpful to pray its lines, asking for trust and for patience that you will experience something of God's faithful love, as the long night gradually gives way to the first streaks of dawn.

Concluding Prayer

Tender-hearted and forgiving God,
you continue to care for me in my darkest moments,
and when I cry to you from the depths of my pain.
Teach me to trust that you are with me always,
especially in the long nights of waiting for some sign of
  dawn.
Help me to recognise the extraordinary nature of
  ordinary blessings,

and to thank you for your faithful love in the details of
    my life.
In faith, hope, and love,
I make this prayer in Jesus' name. Amen.

6 I Thirst!

Psalms of Seeking God

When you look at a photo of a desert, what comes to mind? An immense tract of sand, a waterless 'beach'? A dry land, dusty and unproductive? But if rain falls on this desert, it quickly produces signs of life, even tiny flowers. This desert can be like you. On some days or even months and years, you may experience that nothing is working for you. You feel arid, as dried out as a desert shrub. Do you thirst for God? Can you even have the strength to desire the One who alone can assuage your parched heart? Using psalms of desire, perhaps you can allow your dryness to become fruitful.

Psalm 63 *Longing for God*

O God, you are my God,
I search eagerly for you.
My soul thirsts for you,
my flesh yearns for you,
in a land parched,
and lifeless, without water.

Thus have I gazed upon you in your holy place,
to see your might and your glory.
For better than life is your faithful love,
my lips declare your praise.
Yes, all my life I will bless you,
and in your name will I lift up my hands.

My soul is satisfied as with a rich feast,
and my mouth praises you with joyful lips,
when I remember you upon my bed,
and meditate on you through the night watches.

For you have always been my help,
and in the shadow of your wings I joyously sing.
My soul holds fast to you,
your right hand supports me.

NOTES ON PSALM 63

I search eagerly: Contained in the Hebrew verb of searching used here is
the word for dawn. This suggests the idea that the psalmist sets out on
a renewed search for God with each new dawn. Alternatively, it could
suggest an early morning time of seeking God.

thirsts for you: Thirst is always more acute than hunger, since the need
of water is the most intense and urgent of all human sustenance needs.
Thirsting for God therefore is central to the spiritual quest.

yearns for you: The Hebrew verb of yearning expresses intense desire,
and, together with the image of thirsting, serves to emphasise the all-
encompassing nature of the psalmist's search for God.

parched: The imagery of a parched land depicted here brings to mind the
wilderness of Judah near the Dead Sea. This terrain is extremely hot, dry,
and very saline. It is especially arid and desolate. Against such a background the metaphor of a parched and weary land is very apt.

gazed upon you: The Hebrew verb used here denotes spiritual perception,
often used in the context of prophetic activity. It refers to the vision of
the heart rather than to that of the eyes.

your holy place: A sanctuary or centre of holiness, it most often referred
to the inner part of the Jerusalem Temple.

to see: The possibility that humans could 'see God' was something that the Old Testament took care to deny (Exodus 33:20). Here it must be taken metaphorically, and not literally.

your glory: This word evokes the mysterious presence of God which rested on the Ark of the Covenant during the exodus through the desert.

better than life: The poet is emphatic that God's covenant love is to be prized above the gift of life itself.

all my life: Such is the poet's sense of God that, having sought and found him, he wants to spend his entire life blessing God.

lift up my hands: The lifting up of hands is a universal symbol of self-giving to God in prayer.

upon my bed: With his mind freed of daily concerns, the psalmist can concentrate his thoughts more directly on God, even through the night watches.

in the shadow of your wings: This wonderfully protective maternal image of God occurs quite often in the psalms, and forms a fitting climax to the movement of this psalm of thirsting for God.

holds fast to you: The verb here denotes commitment and loyalty. It is the verb used to describe Ruth's decision to remain with Naomi through thick and thin (Ruth 1:14).

Your right hand supports me: God's right hand is a metaphor for God's ongoing support and strength for the psalmist as he seeks to put God first in his life.

Suggestions for Praying with Psalm 63

The dominant theme in this psalm is one of seeking God. The imagery of thirsting in an arid wilderness is powerful. Nevertheless, the overall mood is confident. The universality of the images makes it possible to pray this psalm on almost any occasion, whether you are feeling close to God or lost in a dry desert. Allow the depths and simplicity of this psalm to draw you into stillness, lingering where you feel God is leading you. A helpful signpost in this thirsting for God might be to ask what can nourish my spirit at this moment of my life's journey.

Concluding Prayer

Most Holy and Awesome God,
deepen my thirst for you.
When I feel parched and weary
draw me into the sanctuary of your faithful love.
Bless me in the silent watches of the night,
and fill me with energy to meet the challenges of
    the new day.
Let my lips tell of your praise,
and may I seek you attentively
in all the encounters of this day.
This prayer I make in the name of Jesus. Amen.

PSALM 42 *Like the Deer*

As the deer cries out for flowing streams,
so my soul cries out for you, O God.
My soul thirsts for God, for the living God.
O when can I enter and see the face of God?

My tears have been my food day and night,
while all day long
people say to me,
'Where is your God?'

Those times I remember,
as I pour out my soul within me:
How I would go with the throng,
leading them in procession to the house of God,

amidst cries of joy and thanksgiving,
with the multitude keeping festival.

Why are you downcast, O my soul,
and why are you in turmoil within me?
Hope in God! for I will still thank him,
my Saviour and my God.

By day the Lord bestows his faithful love,
and at night his song is with me,
a prayer to the God of my life.

I say to God, my Rock,
'Why have you forgotten me?
Why must I go like a mourner
because of the enemy's oppression?'

Why are you downcast, O my soul,
and why are you in turmoil within me?
Hope in God, for I will still thank him,
my Saviour and my God.

NOTES ON PSALM 42

cries out: In Hebrew, as in English, there are specific verbs describing the
sounds peculiar to individual animals: the lion roars, the bear growls,
the cattle low, the bird chirps, and the deer cries. The verb denoting the
deer's unique cry is repeated in the second line as a metaphor for the
psalmist's crying out for God.

flowing streams: This phrase refers to the deepest part of a valley flowing
with fresh water.

enter and see the face of God: The context here is that of pilgrimage to the Jerusalem Temple, and the desire to enter into the holy place or sanctuary so as to experience some sense of God's presence.

My tears: It quickly becomes clear that the psalmist has a motive for his longing. His tears point to some kind of inner turmoil, and a sense of abandonment by God.

Where is your God? This inner state is made all the more bitter because of harassment from people who continually taunt the psalmist with mocking questions as to where is his God. The imagery of 'tears day and night' might imply some form of mourning or sadness.

Those times I remember: In this state of distress he recalls happier times, when his sense of God energised him in his leadership role.

Why are you downcast? In the verses which follow there is no clear dividing line between the expressions of trust and thanksgiving on the one hand, and lament on the other. Some of the images and refrains are repeated or echoed.

Hope in God: The psalmist moves swiftly from lament and despair, to trust, and then to thanksgiving, all in one verse.

By day the Lord bestows his faithful love: The poet then expresses trust in God, whose loving kindness accompanies him day and night.

Why have you forgotten me? The mood of thanksgiving gives way swiftly again, as he returns to the lament mode, and directly questions God, his Rock, as to why he is in such a plight.

I will again thank him: Echoing sentiments already present in the psalm, the author concludes on a note of thanksgiving, resigned to wait for God, and resolved to thank God in spite of all that has happened to him.

Suggestions for Praying with Psalm 42

If you feel alienated or distant from God, do not allow yourself to be overwhelmed. Instead, turn back to God with trust, like the thirsty deer goes in search of a spring of pure water. You too can encounter God anew, and allow his presence fill you with joy. The deer's cry evokes a focused search for water. We may at times go astray, and lose focus as we try to cope with the pressures of modern living. We may wonder where is our God in this turmoil. Let us not be downcast, but with the psalmist, let us take heart from the memory of better times, and trust that God's faithful love cannot change.

Concluding Prayer

Almighty God of creation and eternity,
as surely as the thirsty deer seeks running streams
draw me to your fountain of living water,
that I may drink deeply and be refreshed.
Alert me to the signs of your beauty all around me,
in nature, and especially in other people.
When I feel downcast and in turmoil, lift me up,
and renew my confidence in your faithful love.
May the memory of happier times encourage me
to trust that your love never changes,
and that you are always close at hand.
I make this prayer in Jesus' name. Amen.

PSALM 84 *How Lovely is Your Dwelling Place!*

How lovely is your dwelling place,
O Lord of hosts!

My soul longs greatly, indeed it yearns
for the courts of the Lord.
My heart and my flesh sing joyfully
to the living God.

Even the sparrow finds a home,
and the swallow a nest for herself,
where she may settle her young,
near your altars, O Lord of hosts,
my King and my God.

How blessed are those who dwell in your house,
forever singing your praise.
Blessed are those who find their strength in you,
in whose heart are the pilgrim pathways.

O Lord God of hosts, hear my prayer,
O God of Jacob, listen!
O God, our shield, see!
Look on the face of your anointed.

Better one day in your courts
than a thousand anywhere else.
No good thing does the Lord withhold
from those who walk uprightly.

O Lord of hosts,
blessed is everyone who trusts in you.

NOTES ON PSALM 84

your dwelling place: The temple in Jerusalem was built about 950 BC, as
the final resting place for the Ark of the Covenant. The Ark was a chest of
acacia wood that contained the two tablets of the Ten Commandments,
and was the symbol of God's continuing presence with his chosen
people from the Exodus journey onward.

Lord of hosts: This frequently-used title of Israel's God evokes images of
the Lord as a divine warrior, acting on behalf of his people, with his

army hosts. Over time these latter lost their military character, and were downgraded to became the angelic hosts.

courts: The psalmist yearns for the temple courtyards, where the crowds would assemble to express their devotion and provide mutual support in their acts of worship.

My heart: For the Hebrews the heart had to do with the intellectual and intuitive faculties which constitute the essence of the human spirit.

my flesh: This referred to the physical aspects of the individual. Taken together heart and flesh express the totality of the experience of expressing joyful praise.

sing joyfully: As harmony increases between the outer and inner aspects of longing for God, the poet bursts forth into one integrated song of praise.

the sparrow: The poet points to the tragic irony that, while the smallest and most insignificant bird could build its home in the temple courts, Israel as a nation was destined to be driven into exile, while its temple lay in ruins.

blessed are those who dwell: This beatitude most likely includes both priests and levites, who derived their livelihood from temple service.

who find their strength in you: This second beatitude concerns a much wider group, the multitudes who drew their strength from participation in the various temple liturgies and sacrificial offerings.

the pilgrim pathways: The Hebrews would try to come in pilgrimage to the Jerusalem Temple for the three great festivals, Passover, Pentecost and Tents. These annual pilgrimages were second nature to them, imprinted on their hearts.

hear ... listen ... see ... look: These four pleas sum up the psalmist's desire to have his prayer heard, namely that he spend time in the courts of the Lord, and experience the living God.

the face of your anointed: At the time of composition, this plea would have referred to the anointed Davidic king, for whom the psalmist is making intercession. The early Christians understood this as foreshadowing Jesus, the Christ or Anointed One.

Better one day: Continuing the theme of delight in being in God's dwelling place, the poet expresses in exaggerated fashion how blessed he is to be in these hallowed courts.

Blessed is everyone who trusts in you: The psalm draws to a close with a final beatitude, with the widest possible application.

Suggestions for Praying with Psalm 84

This psalm celebrates the joy of arriving at a pilgrimage's end. Its main focus is on the beauty of God's dwelling place, and the praise that flows from a shared experience of God's presence. Many of its images reflect Old Testament temple practices, rooted in a different culture. But it is possible to make adaptations so that today's believer can exploit the richness of this psalm, and draw strength from it.

God's dwelling place admits of many possibilities. God is not limited to 'holy places', yet some locations in our experience are invested with a sacred quality. Momentarily turning aside from the hustle and bustle of modern life, we are attracted there to focus more fully on God. Yet God cannot be more present in one place and less in another, since God is indivisible. God's presence is universal, and can be symbolised in many ways. God exists in every one of us, in every step, in every breath, and not just in sacred places.

God has not composed a symphony to be played and directed from some distant point in space. God is the symphony that resounds throughout the universe. All we have to do is to resonate with God — sounding as few discordant notes as possible. The imagery in this psalm can transcend the centuries to allow us to become ever more mindful of God's presence in our lives. Resonating with the divine symphony we can be helped to find our strength in God, the living God.

Concluding Prayer

All-powerful and ever present God,
whose gentle presence has enfolded me
since the moment you created me,
draw me more and more into loving awareness of you,
so that I may always find my strength in you.
Teach me to love the beauty of your dwelling place,
and to recognise it all around me,
in majestic mountains and ocean depths,
in tiny flowers and fledgling sparrows,
and especially in the pilgrims
who accompany me on life's journey.
This prayer I make through Jesus, your Anointed One.
   Amen.

Psalm 143 *Like Thirsty Earth*

O Lord, hear my prayer,
give ear to my pleading.
Answer me in your constancy,
in your saving justice.

For enemies have pursued me,
they have crushed my life into the ground.
They have made me sit in darkness,
like those long dead.

I remember back to the days of old,
I reflect on all you have done.
I ponder the works of your hands.
I stretch out my hands to you,
my soul longs for you like thirsty earth.

Answer me quickly, O Lord!
My spirit can endure no more.
Do not hide your face from me,
or I shall become like those who go down into the Pit.

Let me learn of your faithful love in the morning,
for in you have I put my trust.
Show me the way I must take,
for to you I entrust my life.

NOTES ON PS 143

hear … give ear: Rashi, the great medieval Jewish commentator, once explained that to hear denotes hearing from a distance, whereas to give ear suggests listening from close by. The psalmist first asks God to hear his prayer, even if he feels far away from God's presence. Then, as the situation deteriorates, God draws closer to listen attentively to the psalmist's desperate plight.

in your constancy: The Hebrew root underlying constancy is also present in the word Amen, both words implying truth, reliability and steadfastness. The psalmist reminds God that, because God is utterly reliable and steadfast, God must answer him. In other words: 'your word is your bond'.

enemies have pursued me: As in many of the psalms, the enemy is unnamed, and almost always anonymous. We never know exactly to whom the psalmist is referring. This quality of anonymity allows for many different kinds of 'enemy', according to the different needs of those praying the psalm.

pursued … crushed … sit in darkness: The enemy's activity always undermines. The verb to pursue in Hebrew can also be rendered as 'persecute'.

I remember ... I reflect ... I ponder: Faced with the debilitating effects of the 'enemy' onslaught, the poet turns to God, and takes courage from the memory of God's faithful love in the past.

I stretch out my hands: This universal image can bring us right back to infancy, and our first steps. Without a parent's hand we fall.

like thirsty earth: As water breathes new life into the parched earth, so God's constancy revitalises the poet.

can endure no more: The psalmist has reached the limits of endurance. Only God can rescue him.

go down into the Pit: This would mean utter extinction, a fate worse than death.

in the morning: Having reached the brink, the psalmist begs God for renewed energy and enlightenment with the coming of dawn.

I entrust my life: The Hebrew idiom here is 'to lift up my soul'. Having expressed a broad range of emotions and a sense of being almost at his wits' end, the psalmist ends on a wonderfully trusting note.

Suggestions for Praying with Psalm 143

Our lives are full of uncertainty and tragedy. It is not easy to cope with the pain and anxiety that sooner or later life throws at us. The 'enemy' lies in wait all around us, both externally and internally. Like the psalmist, you need to know that God is listening to you, and is close at hand, as you bring your parched spirit to the wellsprings of God's constancy.

When in the thick of hard times it can be helpful to follow the lead of this psalm author. First, ask God to listen to your plea for help. It would be good if you could put words on what lies at the heart of your distress. Then spend some time recalling God's faithful love in the past events of your life. Identify one or two key moments and let the memory of these provide an anchor of hope in the midst of the storm. Like the psalmist, reflect also on God's attention to the minutest details of creation, and then ponder on the wonder of how God is at work in the unfolding of your own life up to the present.

Now, renew your petition, again following the psalmist. You might even want to echo his words, 'my spirit can endure no more'. Finally, using the last verse of the psalm, entrust yourself fully to God. Abandon your life into God's loving hands, and lift up the inner eyes of your spirit in gratitude.

Concluding Prayer

God of unlimited blessings and ever-constant Friend,
in the midst of life's uncertainties and pain
your goodness surrounds my life
and blesses me day after day.
Awaken in my memory the many ways
you have repeatedly blessed my life in the past.
May the power of memory energise me
to go forth this day in the certain knowledge
that I can trust in your constancy and personal
    love for me.
Ease my thirst in my desert moments
and show me the way you want me to take.
I make this prayer in the name of Jesus, Saviour and
    Friend. Amen.

7   I Surrender!

Psalms of Trust

For most people life is a long journey, with varying possibilities. Sometimes the path is smooth and the visibility
excellent. At such times you may not even feel the need of
a guide, as you confidently stride ahead. But there are other
times, however, when you seem to move as in a fog, with no
idea of whether your steps are on solid ground or not. You
may feel that you are never too far from misfortune – an
accident, sickness, unemployment, or family problems. In
such cases you will experience the need of protection and
a safe haven. Who can you trust in the labyrinth of life? At
a human level, a trusty friend, a life-companion or spouse,
is a rare and beautiful gift. But you cannot hold on to such
treasures indefinitely. They too are mortal and their hold on
life is fragile. There is only one enduring person who will
always there for you: God is your refuge and your strength.
Trust God fully.

PSALM 23   *The Lord is my Shepherd*

The Lord is my shepherd,
I lack for nothing.
He lets me rest in green meadows.

Alongside tranquil waters he leads me.
He restores my spirit.
He guides me along upright paths
as befits his name.

Though I walk through a valley of deep darkness, ·
I fear no harm,
for you are with me.
Your rod and your staff – they comfort me.

You spread a table before me
in full view of my tormentors.
You anoint my head with oil,
my cup brims over.

May only goodness and faithful love pursue me
all the days of my life,
and may I dwell in the house of the Lord
for many long years.

NOTES ON PSALM 23

my shepherd: This metaphor describes God as the One who satisfies all human needs. A shepherd trudges about all day, and in all kinds of weather. But, however dedicated a human shepherd may be, by comparison God's care in watching over the psalmist is far superior. A strong biblical symbol of total commitment, this image of shepherd reached its deepest significance when applied to Jesus in the gospel tradition.

I lack for nothing: A genuine shepherd would never allow his sheep to go hungry or to suffer harm of any kind. These words convey the poet's unqualified trust in God's boundless generosity to him.

He lets me rest: The Hebrew verb can also be rendered as 'he makes me lie down'.

green meadows: The poet continues his description of God as a shepherd, likening him to one who seeks out lush grazing pastures for his flock.

tranquil waters: The waters of a tranquil stream are clear and sweet, whereas those of a torrential river are opaque and muddy.

he leads: In the Middle East, even still today, the shepherd goes ahead of his flock and leads them forth each morning to wherever the day's pastures are to be found.

He guides: A further emphasis on God's caring presence, keeping a watchful eye on the sheep, so that he does not tire them unduly by taking them on difficult or roundabout routes.

along upright paths: The meaning here is not simply that of correct routes, but rather refers to 'paths of justice' or paths that are morally upright.

as befits his name: God's 'name' is the phrase the psalmist uses when he wants to speak of God's very being, or essence.

a valley of deep darkness: This image of impenetrable gloom conjures up a place of danger, a ravine as dark and forbidding as the grave itself.

no harm: This can refer to both physical danger and moral evil.

For you are with me: The speaker's trust in God is so strong that he knows that God will always stand by him in times of need. This confidence is further underlined by the fact that he now addresses God directly, changing from the third person in the first seven lines to 'you' in the next six.

Your rod and your staff: The former symbolises correction, while the latter stands for support. The Hebrew word for staff comes from a verb meaning 'to lean upon'.

my tormentors: These represent the psalmist's personal adversaries.

You anoint: Physical anointings with oil carried important symbolic meanings in the biblical tradition. The most important of these was anointing with oil so as to set apart an object or person to God. Here, the psalmist senses that he is being specially chosen and protected by God.

my cup brims over: This is a metaphor describing contentment. God's provisions are not meagre, but are generously given.

only: The psalmist prefaces his request with the diminutive 'only', that is, a small amount, to emphasise that he only asks for the bare minimum.

dwell: The final request is for semi-permanent dwelling in God's house, in the Jerusalem Temple. The speaker is gladly prepared to live in this house of 'goodness and faithful love', and would not want to live anywhere else.

Suggestions for Praying with Psalm 23

Of all the psalms in the Bible this one is by far the most popular. Although used by many believers who may never have met a real shepherd, or whose only contact with sheep or lamb is at the dinner table, the underlying metaphor continues to be an endless reservoir of significance. A true metaphor lives in the struggle between the 'is' and the 'is not'. The Lord is indeed an all-caring and utterly trust-worthy shepherd. But we are constantly stretched to move beyond the literal sense of shepherd, to the 'is not' of the metaphor. This 'is not' invites us into the deepest mystery of a loving God, which lies beyond the power of metaphor or indeed of imagination.

This is a psalm for all seasons and for all believers. Its powerful sense of trust pervades each verse. In a consumer-driven society which thrives on our need to have, the opening line is both strong and simple. Can you honestly say that, with the Lord as your shepherd, you really lack for nothing? Try it! As the psalm unfolds, the poet moves from a third-person description of God to direct speech. It's as if, having accepted that God does really care, the psalmist can now address God directly. He can now risk total surrender in situations of greatest need, whether floundering in a deep valley of distress, or trying to cope with 'tormentors', inter-nal or external. The final stanza reaffirms the atmosphere of serene trust with which the psalm opened.

One way of praying with this psalm would be to move slowly and lovingly through each line, pausing where it seems appropriate, and allowing yourself to experience the psalm's conviction and simplicity. Or, if you are in that valley of deep distress, pray for the trust and courage to believe that God is with you even there, and will safely guide you to 'tranquil waters'.

Concluding Prayer

God of Mystery, and Shepherd of my soul,
your holiness surrounds and permeates all that I am.
You lead me to green pastures,
and refresh me with calm waters.
Even when I stumble through valleys of darkness
set me free from all fear.
With your beckoning whispers
and your staff which supports,
guide my soul along upright paths.
Grant me to dwell in your loving presence
today and forever. Amen.

PSALM 131 *Like a Trusting Child*

O Lord, my heart is not proud,
nor are my eyes haughty.
I do not pursue important matters,
nor issues beyond me.

Rather, I have stilled and hushed my soul
like a weaned child upon its mother's lap.
Like a weaned child upon me is my soul.

**Let Israel wait for the Lord
from this time forth and forever.**

NOTES ON PSALM 131

my heart is not proud: The heart symbolises the inner depths of the person. This inner sanctum is where proud thoughts can be harboured.

nor are my eyes haughty: By contrast, the eyes represent the exterior aspect of the person, and how one's eyes can view others arrogantly.

important matters ... issues beyond me: The poet affirms that his preferences and ambitions have always been simple and humble.

stilled and hushed: In spiritual matters the poet is like an innocent child who sleeps peacefully, secure in the arms of its mother.

Like a weaned child: A weaned toddler has achieved some measure of independence, yet it hovers beside its mother, for she is still its indispensable source of security, guidance and support.

Let Israel wait: Moving from personal reflection, the speaker now applies the metaphor of childlike trust to the nation as a whole. Israel must learn the art of waiting for the Lord, and that political and military affairs will not of themselves bring salvation.

Suggestions for Praying with Psalm 131

A top of the range car, clothes in the latest fashion, influential friends. Are these sufficient to satisfy the aspirations of your heart? The clear message of this psalm points elsewhere. God is all that the human heart longs for. Since God has created the human heart, he knows it through and through, all its deepest needs. At the core of this psalm lies a powerful image: the simplicity of a trusting child resting on its mother's lap. The infant does not need to do anything to earn its mother's love. Resting there in quietness, it knows that it is cherished. Choose some of the key words in this short psalm which will help to calm you, as you allow the simplicity of its imagery suggest how you might pray.

Concluding Prayer

Great caring and inviting God,
bless me with joy and peace in my living this day.
Let there be moments of childlike wonder in my heart.
Teach me how to be quiet,
so that in stillness I may hear your word.
Lift me up in your loving arms,
and draw me ever more deeply
into the mystery of your holiness.
This prayer I make in the name of Jesus,
my Saviour and Guide. Amen.

PSALM 139 (1) *God Knows*

As each new generation enters the stage of history, it follows an ancient script as the divine drama unfolds. God knows everything, yet women and men retain varying levels of freedom to follow their individual paths in life. This psalm captures the poet's overwhelming sense of awe in pondering God's providential guidance of human affairs. People of faith follow life's path willingly, for they travel with God in a trusting relationship of love. This psalm unfolds in three movements: (i) God knows, (ii) God is ever present, (iii) God invites a response. Each of the three sections has its own coherence within the overall unity of the psalm.

O Lord, you search me and you know!
You know when I sit and when I stand.
You understand my thoughts from afar.

My journey and my resting you watch over,
with all my ways you are familiar.
Even when a word is not yet on my tongue,
you, O Lord, know it completely.

You encircle me behind and before,
and rest your hand upon me.
Such knowledge is too wonderful for me,
it is so lofty, I cannot fathom it.

NOTES ON PSALM 139 (I)

you search me: The basic meaning of this verb is 'to be deep'. It is used in
the Bible both of humans searching out hidden or mysterious things,
and of God's capacity to see into the human heart.

and you know: There is no direct object after this verb in the original
Hebrew, even though many translations insert one: 'and you know me'.
As it stands, it is more powerful, signaling God's omniscience. God is
the One who simply knows.

when I sit and when I stand: God is keenly aware of every shift in my
posture, all my external movements.

You understand my thoughts: God effortlessly discerns also what is inter-
nal, deep within me.

My journey and my resting: God watches over both my active and passive
routines, that is, God watches over me totally.

you are familiar: This verb carries the sense of 'being intimately
acquainted with'.

not yet on my tongue: As in Jeremiah 1:5, 'Before I formed you in the
womb I knew you', God knows every detail of my life before I was born.

You encircle me: The Hebrew verb usually means 'to besiege, hem in'. In
this context, where the poet celebrates God's protective watchfulness,
the sense of 'encircling' is more fitting.

rest your hand: The touch of God's hand is experienced as caring and
  protective.
too wonderful: The psalmist is overwhelmed when trying to grasp God's
  omniscience. It is totally beyond his comprehension.
so lofty, I cannot fathom it: The poet's choice of words shows how this
  mysterious knowledge of God is both too elevated and too deep for him.

Suggestions for Praying with Psalm 139 (1)

God knows you totally, whether you are sitting or standing, rising or resting. God knows you better than you know
yourself. Sometimes this may be of concern to you, and at
other times, it becomes a great source of trust and security.
Just as children feel safe and secure because they know that
their parents love them, so you can grow into ever deeper
trust that God loves you unconditionally. At times it can
be very difficult to accept this unconditional love, but the
psalm assures us that God's protective hand rests on us, to
encircle us with love. It can be helpful to focus on what it
feels like to accept that God knows us through and through
and still loves us. Notice how often the idea of 'knowing'
occurs in this first part of the psalm. What does it feel like to
be known and loved in this way?

Concluding Prayer

All-knowing and caring God,
you are ever with me in my rising and resting,
in my joys and sorrows.
Continue to encircle me in your protective care
and shield me from taking the wrong path.
Your intimate knowledge of me is beyond my grasp,
but I trust in you totally.
Through the hours of this day walk with me,
and when night comes,

watch over me and grant me to sleep securely,
in the certainty of your unconditional love.
This prayer I make in the name of Jesus. Amen.

PSALM 139 (II)   *God is Ever Present*

Where can I go from your spirit?
From your presence where can I flee?
If I scale the heavens, you are there,
if I lie flat in Sheol, there you are!

If I take the wings of dawn
and bed down at the farthest limits of the sea,
even there your hand would guide me,
and your right hand hold me fast.

If I say, 'Surely darkness will envelop me,
and the light around me become night,'
even darkness is not too dark for you,
and night is as luminous as the day.
For darkness and light are but one.

NOTES ON PSALM 139 (II)

where can I flee: The futility of hiding from God's presence can be traced
    through Jonah, right back to the first couple in the Genesis garden.

scale the heavens…lie flat in Sheol: There is no extreme location beyond
    God's presence.

the wings of dawn: At the crack of dawn, the first rays of sunlight begin
    to spread across the expanse of the horizon like a mighty bird spreading
    its shining wings. Even if the poet had wings and could fly as fast as the
    spreading light of a new day, he would not escape God's presence. The

dazzling light envelops the earth, just as God's all-pervasive presence encompasses the entire globe.

your hand would guide me: Even if the poet succeeded in fleeing to the most remote reaches of the earth, he would still need God's guiding hand.

right hand: A symbol for God's kindness, mercy and strength.

night is as luminous as the day: Even darkness provides no shelter from the Almighty's penetrating vision, giving further evidence of the futility of attempting to hide from God.

Suggestions for Praying with Psalm 139 (II)

Consciously or unconsciously we are immersed in God's presence. Like the sun, even if we turn away from it, and cast our gaze on earthly objects, it is still the sun which gives these objects all their colours, and allows us to see them. Also at night, it is the same sun that gives light to the moon and stars. And the clouds which occasionally hide the sun can only be seen by us because they are penetrated by the sun's light.

To live immersed in this wonderful presence of God should be as natural to us as to drink in the benefits of the sun. Without the sun we would be lost. Without God, we would be cut off even more radically from our source of life.

By becoming more and more aware of the divine presence in your heart, you can become increasingly aware of that same divine presence surrounding you on all sides. God is fully present everywhere. God does not change, and does not 'come' or 'go' from one place to another. Everywhere and always God is. There is no sense in which God can be 'more' here or 'less' there. Allow the poetry of this part of the psalm to speak to you of the constancy of God's loving presence in your life, in all its moments.

Concluding Prayer

Wonderful God of time and eternity,
you are more present to me than I am to myself.
I thank you for the gift of life,
and for your gracious care of me at every moment.
May I become ever more aware
that all that is human is your creation, and thus holy.
Before you my life is transparent.
Move me at the depths of my being
so that I may grow to love your precious designs,
and that I may become the person you invite me to be.
This prayer I make in love and gratitude. Amen.

PSALM 139 (III)   *God Invites a Response*

You it was who formed my inmost being,
you knit me together in my mother's womb.
I thank you, for I am awesomely, wondrously made.
Wondrous are your works – that I know very well.

My frame was not hidden from you,
when I was being made in secret,
embroidered in the depths of the earth.

Your eyes could see my unformed embryo.
In your book were all written the days
that were shaped before one of them came to be.

How precious to me are your designs, O God!
How vast the sum of them!

If I could count them – they would outnumber the
  sand,
When I awake – I am still with you.

NOTES ON PSALM 139 (III)

my inmost being: The Hebrew word used here is 'kidneys'. These symbol-
  ise the seat of innermost thought, hidden deep within the human frame.
  God's vision penetrates even here.

You knit me together: This beautiful image portrays God as a weaver,
  fashioning the poet within the hidden depths of his mother's womb.
  God is even present and active there.

I thank you: This extended reflection on the mystery of God's creative
  presence in the poet's life from conception onwards leads to an outburst
  of gratitude.

I am awesomely, wondrously made: Even the most elementary study of
  human anatomy fills the poet with wonder and awe at the marvels of
  creation. Human beings are at the pinnacle of this creation.

My frame: My skeletal structure, or my potential metaphorically speaking, was not hidden from you.

embroidered: The human body is an extremely complex organism, woven
  together in a vast array of bones, muscles, sinews, tendons and tissues.
  The psalmist tries to capture the harmony of this complexity through
  the imagery of embroidery, and stresses that all of this complexity is not
  beyond God's creative energy.

my unformed embryo: The Hebrew word describes an unshaped mass,
  such as a block of wood or a chunk of clay, which has not yet been fashioned into a vessel. When an embryo is conceived, it has the potential of
  all its future limbs and organs. God however sees in advance the fully-
  shaped human that will emerge from this unshaped form, and knows
  how this tiny embryo will realise its potential in the days and years
  which lie ahead.

How precious: God's plans for creation are splendid and awesome.

If I could count them: The psalmist tries to convey some sense of the
countless purposeful designs that God has incorporated into creation.

When I awake: The poet, captivated by the sheer immensity of the
wonders of creation, awakes as if from a dream.

I am still with you: The poet's response to the beauty of God's creation is
one of trust and commitment.

Suggestions for Praying with Psalm 139 (iii)

God has a purpose and a plan for everything in creation. If
you believe that God has a purpose for you personally, it will
affect the way you live and love. God's love for you goes back
to when you were an 'unformed embryo'. Such enduring
love in your life invites a response. The words of this section
of the psalm would be especially apt to use on your birthday.
What better day is there on which to celebrate that you have
been 'awesomely, wondrously made'? Can you spend some
time rejoicing in the fact that God has fashioned you in the
womb, embroidering you into the wonderful person that
you now are? You are truly God's work of art.

Concluding Prayer

O Beauty ever ancient, ever new,
you have been with me since the moment of my
    conception,
and you continue to guide me still.
You embroidered me in the depths of my mother's
    womb,
so your designs are precious to me.
I thank you for the wonder of all creation,
and especially for the wonder of my being.
Enable me today to see my life as a gift,
a gift given in trust from you.

In all of my work and play
may your grace bless me and make me whole.
I make this prayer in the name of the triune God. Amen.

8 Let's Celebrate!

Psalms of Thanksgiving

The psalms mirror various attitudes in prayer that we can relate to today. In the choice of psalms explored up to this point you may have noticed that the focus has been largely on the individual praying, and on her/his need. When we turn to this next group the spotlight changes. In the psalms of thanksgiving attention shifts from the individual and onto God, who now becomes centre stage.

With great enthusiasm ancient Israel celebrated both its creator and the wonders of creation. Thanksgiving played a central part in this worship. Festival processions on the way to Jerusalem filled the air with 'glad shouts and songs of thanksgiving' (Psalm 42:4), as all the tribes of Israel went up to the holy city in pilgrimage 'to give thanks to the name of the Lord' (Psalm 122:4).

Even if many of the thanksgiving psalms are formulated in the first person, as though expressing the gratitude of one individual, they were mainly composed for communal liturgy, and have come down to us precisely because of being channelled in a liturgical setting from one generation to the next. Because they were composed for a communal setting, it is not possible to discover in detail the circumstances that gave rise to the thanksgiving. Where these exist, they are often expressed in general terms. This lack of precision was possibly the secret of their adaptability, a feature that makes it possible for us to continue to use them today to express our gratitude.

PSALM 92 *It is Good to Give Thanks*

It is good to give thanks to the Lord,
to sing psalms to your name, O Most High,
to declare your faithful love at daybreak,
and your steadfastness each night,
on a ten-stringed harp,
to the sounding chords of the lyre.

For you have gladdened me, O Lord, by your deeds,
at the works of your hands I shout for joy.
How great are your works, O Lord!
How deep are your designs!

A senseless person cannot know this,
a fool cannot grasp it:
though the wicked sprout like grass
though all evildoers blossom,
they are destined for eternal destruction,
but you are exalted, O Lord, for all time.

The just will flourish like the palm tree,
and thrive like a cedar in Lebanon.
Planted in the house of the Lord,
they will flourish in the courts of our God.

They will still be fruitful in old age,
full of sap and freshness they will be,
declaring that the Lord is upright,
my Rock, in whom there is no wrong.

NOTES ON PSALM 92

to give thanks ... to sing psalms: The mood of this thanksgiving psalm
is particularly positive. Its opening lines illustrate the typical rhyming
of ideas which characterises biblical poetry. The two verbs balance each
other, being two ways in which gratitude spills over into action.

your faithful love ... your steadfastness: These characteristics associated
with God often occur in tandem, and complement each other.

at daybreak ... each night: The citing of dawn and dusk draws attention
to the non-stop quality of God's reliability.

ten-stringed harp ... lyre: Both are stringed instruments, the former
having ten strings giving forth ten different notes.

you have gladdened me ... I shout for joy: Again, the poetic balance in
these two statements conveys the poet's mood of joyful thanksgiving.

your works ... your designs: The speaker first identifies in a general way
the reason for the thanksgiving. God's two outstanding mighty works
are creation and liberation from slavery in Egypt.

A senseless person ... a fool cannot grasp it: The poet now uses negative
images to develop the argument that God is so worthy of thanksgiving
that only a stupid person cannot or will not see this.

palm tree: The date palm is a magnificent, tall tree that grows abundantly
in the Near East. Its large leaves radiate from the top of a single trunk
that can grow to more than fifteen metres. In the Bible the palm tree
appears as a symbol of grandeur and steadfastness, as is the case here.

a cedar in Lebanon: The celebrated cedars of Lebanon are large, conifer-
ous, evergreen mountain trees, aptly named, as they did not grow in
Israel. The psalmist compares the growth of the righteous to that of the
lofty cedars of Lebanon.

flourish in the courts: It is very likely that this thanksgiving psalm
was composed for Israel's communal celebrations in the courts of the
Jerusalem Temple.

fruitful even in old age: The metaphor grows beyond the normal fertility-
cycle, in that the just can continue to bear fruit past usual expectations,
and into old age.

full of sap and freshness: An encouraging image for an older age group, it
  also reflects the respect shown to older people in the Bible.

my Rock: Among the many biblical metaphors used for God, this one
  evokes durability, permanence and the utmost reliability.

Suggestions for Praying with Psalm 92

When you were a toddler, among the first words you were
most likely taught to say were 'thank you'. Why? Because
your parents knew instinctively that a grateful approach to
life can transform the ordinary exchanges of every day into
blessings. G.K. Chesterton once wrote, 'You say grace before
meals. All right. But I say grace before the concert and the
opera, and grace before the play and pantomime, and grace
before I open a book, and grace before sketching, painting,
swimming, fencing, boxing, walking, playing, dancing and
grace before I dip the pen in the ink.'

It is a truism that life does not always deal you the cards
you would like. However, choosing to look for what is good
in every situation can help you to see how your life could
be filled with gratitude. An appreciative approach to life is
contagious. It's often called 'counting your blessings'!

The movement of this psalm is one of joyful appreciation. The poet knows from experience and with the eyes of
faith that 'it is good to give thanks to God'. The motives for
giving thanks are then spelled out. Because of God's faithful
love and steadfastness the psalmist can spontaneously break
forth into joyful gratitude. When you pray with this psalm it
might be helpful if you identify some personal reasons why
you too can say 'it is good to give thanks to God'.

Concluding Prayer

God of abundance and endless generosity,
thank you for your faithful love at daybreak,

and your gentle care at night.
Thank you for the countless ways
you lighten my burdens and grace my path.
Teach me to appreciate the generosity of others
and to remember always to thank them.
May I have a song of praise in my heart
and the quiet joy of a life lived in gratitude.
In the name of Jesus, my Saviour and Friend
I make this prayer. Amen.

PSALM 124 *With the Lord on Our Side*

Were it not for the Lord, who was on our side,
let Israel now declare,
were it not for the Lord, who was on our side,
when people rose against us,

Then would they have swallowed us alive,
as their fury blazed against us.
Then the waters would have inundated us,
the torrent would have surged over us,
then over us would have surged the raging waters.

Blessed be the Lord, who did not hand us over
as prey to their teeth.
We have escaped with our lives,
like a bird from the snare of the hunters.
The snare is broken, and we have escaped.

Our help is in the name of the Lord,
who made heaven and earth.

NOTES ON PSALM 124

Were it not for the Lord: The opening lines introduce an imaginary but credible situation of personal danger. They hint at what might have been, had the Lord been 'absent'.

who was on our side: Voicing the concerns of the community rather than those of an individual, this psalm develops its theme through a growing opposition between 'us' and 'them'.

swallowed us alive … their fury blazed: The danger is initially depicted in images of being devoured by the enemy's uncontrollable anger.

the waters would have inundated us: The poet now uses the imagery of flood waters, deploying a variety of terms that evoke the kinds of devastation caused by tsunamis in recent times.

surged over us: The repetition of this phrase underlines the helplessness of a community when caught up in a tidal wave, or other forms of flooding.

Blessed be the Lord: The poet now moves from what might have been to what actually happened. The Lord is to be blessed and thanked because the community has been spared catastrophe.

as prey to their teeth: The imagery now moves from natural disasters to those caused by human despoilers, whose chief aim is to entrap and kill their prey.

escaped … escaped: The relief is palpable, as the poet repeats the verb for emphasis.

like a bird: There is a dramatic contrast between being pulled downward into raging waters and the upward flight of an escaping bird, a symbolic contrast between the elements of death and life.

snare … snare: Repetition again underscores the enormity of the danger that has been averted, thanks to the Lord's provident care.

Our help is in the name of the Lord: The final stanza affirms the Lord's creative power over heaven and earth, guaranteeing that those who trust in God will receive the strength to cope with any danger.

Suggestions for Praying with Psalm 124

The Psalms often speak of 'enemies'. Do you know who or what is your greatest enemy? Perhaps it is self-centeredness, or a false love of the self? On your own you cannot escape the many snares of egotism. But with the Lord you can learn to overcome some of them. We cannot be victorious all the time, but we can learn to trust that God is with us and on our side no matter how dark the horizon.

There is a deeper question underlying this psalm. What does it mean to have God on our side when we are crushed and in pain? When we feel trapped or drowning? Learning how to express gratitude when life is difficult and uncertain can challenge our natural tendency towards self-absorption. It can lift us out of our egotism.

'If the only prayer you say in your life is thank you, that would suffice' (Meister Eckhart).

Concluding Prayer

Ever-present and caring God,
you are my constant companion
in the twists and turns of life's journey.
Through the hours of this day
walk with me in each of my several paths.
I thank you for the countless times
you have saved me from the raging waters.
I beg you to break the snares that entrap me
and that keep me imprisoned in selfishness.
I also ask you for the courage and strength
to confront my inner demons.
Knowing that my help is in the name of the Lord,
I make this prayer beneath the cross of Jesus. Amen.

PSALM 111 *With All my Heart*

Hallelujah!
I give thanks to the Lord with all my heart,
in the gathering of the upright, in the assembly.
Great are the works of the Lord,
pondered over by all who delight in them.

His deeds are full of majesty and splendour.
His righteousness stands firm forever.
He has gained renown by his wonderful deeds,
the Lord is gracious and tenderness.

He provides food for those who fear him,
he keeps his covenant always in mind.
He has shown his people the power of his works,
giving them the heritage of the nations.

The works of his hands are truth and justice,
reliable are all his decrees.
They are established forever and ever,
to be performed with loyalty and uprightness.

The fear of the Lord is the beginning of wisdom,
prudent are all who practise it.
His praise endures forever.

NOTES ON PSALM 111

Hallelujah: This invitation to 'Praise the Lord' shows how biblical expressions of thanks and praise blend into each other seamlessly. Praise and thanks are two sides of the same coin, and are essentially inseparable, as in the case of this psalm.

I give thanks: A clear statement of purpose identifies the speaker's mood of gratitude.

with all my heart: The poet expresses his desire to give thanks enthusiastically and with an unconditional outpouring of all that he is.

in the gathering ... in the assembly: These two locations give an unambiguous insight as to why psalms were composed, and how they were used. The support of a large number of like-minded worshippers would have given an extraordinary energy to these shared acknowledgements of God's faithfulness and love.

Great are the works of the Lord: The reasons for gratitude at these liturgical gatherings were linked first and foremost with the works of the Lord. In the Bible these are simplified into two great categories: God's mighty acts associated with Exodus and those associated with Creation. Ancient Israel came to know its God first of all through the historical experience of liberation from Egypt. Growth in insight into God's wonderful deeds led them to recognise their God as creator of the universe, as the first and the last, as unique and incomparable.

pondered over: The Hebrew verb here refers to how one should search the Scriptures, and study them in depth, so as to be able to express wonder and gratitude to God. This prayerful pondering provides a model that has stood the test of time. Throughout the Christian centuries, and into the present, the practice of *lectio divina* continues to open up the hidden treasures of the Bible in a fruitful and personal manner.

delight in them: Reflection on God's wonderful works cannot but result in joyfulness.

The Lord is gracious and tenderness: Although God's deeds are awesome, yet God is also approachable, full of kindness and compassion.

He provides food: As creator, God is celebrated in the Bible as the ultimate provider of all things necessary for survival and everyday life.

those who fear him: The fear implied here is one of reverence and awe, not that of cringing before a powerful and angry deity.

covenant always in mind: God is to be thanked because he is faithful and utterly trustworthy. His word can be counted upon, and his love is unconditional.

reliable are all his decrees: The remainder of the psalm illustrates why the worshippers would want to thank God.

The fear of the Lord is the beginning of wisdom: As earlier in the psalm, here too the fear of the Lord is to be seen as awe-filled insight into this mysterious God. This kind of approach constitutes true wisdom.

Suggestions for Praying with Psalm III

It may come as a surprise to realise that most days we receive much more than we give. Sometimes when our light goes out it is blown into flame again by a seemingly chance encounter with another person. We owe a debt of gratitude to those who kindle this inner light. 'I have walked this earth for thirty years', wrote Vincent van Gogh, 'and, out of gratitude, I want to leave some souvenir.'

The opening line of Psalm III brims over with gratitude, and sets the tone for what follows. Notice that the focus throughout the psalm is fully on God as the one to be thanked and appreciated for all good gifts. The poet delights in the various reasons why God is to be thanked. Allow yourself some space to notice some of the giftedness in your life, as you ponder 'the works of the Lord'. Give thanks to God with a full heart for what you have experienced as good. Pray also for the courage to accept those things that you find difficult, trusting that in God's providence you may understand one day why they form part of your journey just now.

Concluding Prayer

God of infinite goodness and generosity,
I come before you to thank you with all my heart
and to praise you for all your gifts.

I thank you for the gift of my life, and for my family.
I thank you for my friends and companions on life's
    journey.
I thank you for your guiding providence each day.
I thank you for goodness encountered in unexpected
    places.
I thank you for the countless glimpses
your creation gives me of your overwhelming beauty.
Above all I thank you for Jesus Christ,
your Son and my Saviour,
in whose name I make this prayer. Amen.

PSALM 118 *Give Thanks to the Lord*

O give thanks to the Lord, for he is good,
for his faithful love endures forever!

In distress I called on the Lord,
the Lord answered me by setting me free.
The Lord is with me, I have no fear.
What can mortals do against me?

It is better to take refuge in the Lord
than to rely on human beings.
It is better to take refuge in the Lord
than to rely on nobles.

I was pushed hard, so that I was falling,
but the Lord came to my help.
The Lord is my strength and my song,
he has become my salvation.

The Lord's right hand is victorious,
the Lord's right hand acts powerfully.
I shall not die, but I shall live,
to recount the deeds of the Lord.

The stone that the builders rejected
has become the cornerstone.
This is the Lord's doing.
It is marvellous in our eyes.

This is the day that the Lord has made,
let us rejoice and be glad in it.
The Lord is God,
and has given us light.

You are my God, and I thank you,
you are my God, and I offer you praise.
O give thanks to the Lord, for he is good,
for his faithful love endures forever!

NOTES ON PSALM 118

give thanks to the Lord, for he is good: The two opening lines identify
the central theme of Psalm 118 as one of thanksgiving. These lines are
repeated at the closing of the psalm. They celebrate two core motives for
gratitude: the Lord's enduring goodness and his faithful love.

In distress ... setting me free: There is a powerful contrast between the
two situations evoked here. The Hebrew word underlying 'distress'
means 'to be hemmed in or snookered', that is, 'to be in a narrow place'.
By contrast the phrase 'setting me free' is an attempt to render the
Hebrew idiom: 'a broad place' (literally, 'the Lord answered me with a
broad place'). The stress which results from suffering and from being in

danger constricts a person's spirit, but God's deliverance creates joy and relief which causes the spirit to expand.

The Lord is with me: This phrase, which occurs often in the psalms, expresses the source of the speaker's trust, the platform from which he can confront danger or enemies. It is the reason why he does not fear what others might do against him.

It is better to take refuge in the Lord: This statement is repeated for emphasis, and continues the theme of trust articulated in the earlier lines.

rely on nobles: Parallel to 'human beings' are these 'nobles' or people belonging to the upper classes to whom one might be tempted to turn for help, instead of the Lord.

but the Lord came to my help: The motive for gratitude becomes more focused: God's help, experienced in a situation of great stress, of 'being pushed hard'.

my strength and my song … my salvation: This refrain is also found in the 'Song of the Sea' at Exodus 15:2, which Moses and all the people sung in celebration after the astonishing crossing of the Reed Sea during their escape from Egypt.

The Lord's right hand: In the Bible God's 'right hand' symbolizes both power and authority.

I shall not die, but I shall live: In the original setting of the psalm these words would have indicated the psalmist's certainty that, with God on his side, he would escape from his enemies who were plotting to kill him. The early Christians would have interpreted these words as referring to Jesus' conquering of death through his resurrection.

The stone that the builders rejected: For its full meaning, this complex metaphor should be linked with Isaiah 28:16. The verse from Isaiah speaks of a foundation stone laid in Zion, 'a tested stone, a precious cornerstone, a sure foundation'. Later Jewish tradition identified David as this stone, who was 'rejected by the builders' in that all of David's older brothers were first presented to Samuel as potential candidates, before the young shepherd boy was eventually chosen to be king. The early Christian communities saw this verse fulfilled in the death and resurrection of Jesus (Matthew 21:42; Acts 4:11; Romans 9:33; Ephesians 2:20; 1 Peter 2:4-8).

the cornerstone: This architectural term most likely describes the keystone of an arched door or gateway, the centre and topmost stone joining the two sides and supporting the arch itself. As such it becomes the most important stone, without which the arch would collapse. Jesus, rejected by his own people, in God's providence becomes the cornerstone of a new people.

This is the Lord's doing: The psalmist again reminds his listeners of the motives for gratitude and celebration.

This is the day that the Lord has made: The atmosphere of gratitude continues for the psalmist as the Lord's marvellous deeds are celebrated in festival. In the Christian tradition this verse is sung at Easter in celebration of Jesus' resurrection.

and has given us light: God is the source of all light, 'and in his light we see light' (see Psalm 36:10).

You are my God: This affirmation of trust is repeated, in combination first with thanks and then with praise. The psalm then concludes as it opened.

Suggestions for Praying with Psalm 118

The dominant theme of Psalm 118 is gratitude to God for deliverance from distress. This sense of deliverance is celebrated in varying ways as the psalm unfolds.

As you become more at home in this psalm you may wish to stay with one or other verse, as seems appropriate to your particular situation. One or two lines may be sufficient to suggest to you how you might express your own gratitude to God for deliverance from distress or for blessings received.

This psalm was particularly familiar to the early Christian community, for in it they found many phrases foreshadowing the suffering, death and resurrection of Jesus. The symbolism of the rejection of the cornerstone was not missed, as they attempted to find meaning in the extraordinary events of Jesus' passion and resurrection.

This tradition of interpreting the psalm in relation to Jesus' death and resurrection has been carried on to the present day through the fact that Psalm 118 is the first psalm of Morning Prayer in the Divine Office on the second and fourth Sunday of each month.

Concluding Prayer

Almighty and Ever-present God,
your love for us is so great
that you gave us your beloved Son Jesus
to be our companion and fellow pilgrim on earth.
He is our cornerstone in life,
our strength, our song and our salvation.
He has shown us how to love, even unto death.
When I am pushed hard and about to give up,
I turn to you, asking for strength and courage
to trust that you are with me,
and that you will never let me be lost.
Within the strong and compassionate arms of Jesus,
I make this prayer. Amen.

9 The Great Hallelujah!

Psalms of Praise

How do you respond when you see the sun rising in all its splendour? Or when you admire a photo of the massive rocky peaks of the Andes or the Alps? Or when you follow the ebb and flow of the tides and seasons? Or wonder at the perfection of a new-born baby? If created things are marvels, how much more marvellous is the creator who has made them all, and has organised them unto their last detail.

In this last choice of psalms we focus on those which have praise of God at their heart. These are the psalms which celebrate the wonder and greatness of God in spontaneous and unselfconscious admiration.

In our consumer-driven world of non-stop advertising, praise becomes devalued. Everything marketable is lauded, whether it be bananas or beer, cameras or crisps. Motor bikes are 'awesome' and ipods are 'must-haves'. Compared with this trivialization of excellence, one may ask if there are any superlatives left for God, who alone is holy. The psalms of praise clearly answer yes! In the words of Thomas Merton, 'the psalms are the best possible way of praising God'. Made up of cries of exultation and wonder, they celebrate God as the source of all goodness. There is much beauty in the psalms to stir up childlike wonder. The God who calls the stars by name, and who stretches out the heavens like a tent, invites us to drink from these streams of delight.

But we sometimes think we don't need this God. Least of all do we think we need to praise him. Lack of interest in the psalms could conceal a lack of interest in God. For if we have no interest in praising God, it might mean that we have never realised who God really is. But when we do come to that awareness, the only possible response is a cry of exultation that comes from the heart, in praise of the One who has done great things for us.

We do not have to be unusual to appreciate the psalms. All that is needed is an open, healthy attitude with a lot of faith and enough freedom from the tastes and prejudices of our time to appreciate the imagery of another culture and age. Entering into these songs of praise allows us experience the emotions they draw forth from the heart. We must sing them to God and make our own all the meaning they contain. Our English word psalm comes from Greek, and means 'a song of praise'.

The songs of praise focus on two chief themes: praise of God as the creator of a wondrous world, and praise of God as the Saviour and Protector of a special people. The more familiar we become with the poetry of these hymns of praise, we will begin to see how it is possible to say, 'My soul sings psalms to God unceasingly' (Psalm 30:12). The height and depth of praise urged on us in the psalms can heighten our sense of marvel and awaken our capacity to appreciate the grandeur of this world.

The gospel tells us that 'where our treasure is there also will be our heart'. The purpose of the psalms is to reveal to us God who is the treasure whom we love, because he first loved us. St Augustine writes that God has taught us to praise him in the psalms, not in order that God might get something out of this praise, but in order that we may be made better by it.

Psalm 8 *How Majestic is Your Name*

O Lord, our God,
how majestic is your name through all the earth!
You have set your splendour above the heavens.

Out of the mouths of babes and infants
you have established strength against your enemies,
to silence the enemy and the avenger.

When I behold your heavens, the work of your fingers,
the moon and the stars that you have set firm,
what are frail mortals that you should remember them,
human beings that you take note of them?

Yet you have made them little less than a god,
crowned them with glory and beauty.
You have given them command
over the works of your hands,
you have put everything at their feet,

All sheep and oxen,
even the beasts of the field,
the birds of the air, the fish of the sea,
and whatever moves along ocean paths.

O Lord, our God,
how majestic is your name through all the earth!

NOTES ON PSALM 8

how majestic: The psalm opens and closes with this exclamatory statement, which the poet utters in amazement.

your name through all the earth: The true essence of God's being is beyond human comprehension. The names and titles we give to God are merely descriptions of the faint glimpses of the divine which God reveals to us through events and through creation. But that tiny glimmer is spectacular.

set your splendour above the heavens: God's splendour is truly 'above' the heavens for humanity is not equipped to appreciate it in all its wonder.

Out of the mouths of babes and infants: This is an enigmatic verse. One possible way of attempting to understand it would be to notice that God's 'strength' or control over creation is evident in even the smallest details on earth. A tiny baby enters the world and instantly, in the very mechanics of its need for food, we witness wonders. Its mother is able to nurse it, with her flow of milk regulated according to the baby's need. Nor does the baby need instruction on how and when to feed.

you have established strength: At this earliest stage of human life outside the womb, a foundation is already established upon which to build a lifetime of recognising God's 'strength', that is, God's amazing presence in and control over every aspect of the universe.

against your enemies: These illustrations of the divine creative power are designed to silence those unwilling to acknowledge God as creator.

When I behold your heavens: After being amazed by God's wondrous works on earth, the poet is now ready to contemplate God's handiwork in the beauty of the night sky.

the work of your fingers: When demonstrating something the finger is used to point out details, leaving no room for ambiguity. The metaphor of God's 'fingers' suggests intricacy of detail and extra care taken to produce the unique diversity of each dissimilar star or heavenly body. Each unique product of God's 'fingers' blends with all the others in one beautiful coordinated whole.

the moon and the stars: During the day the sun is so bright that it does not allow us to see the vastness of the universe. But at night, as the earth recedes into the shade, the starry hosts of luminous worlds become visible to the human eye. Then earth shrinks to a mere speck in this universe, and we humans inhabiting this speck become very tiny indeed, even smaller specks.

what are frail mortals: This question lies at the heart of the psalm. As the poet loses himself in admiration of these amazing celestial bodies, an even greater wonder takes hold of him.

that you should remember them ... take note of them? Conscious of his mortality when contrasted with the enduring character of the heavenly bodies, the poet comes to a wonderful personal realisation: at the heart of this great universe he is nevertheless the special object of God's love.

little less than a god ... with glory and beauty: The psalm becomes a psalm of praise to God, who so loves these frail mortals that he crowns them with wonderful freedom and dignity.

you have put everything at their feet: This 'everything' is expanded into a brief summary: domestic and wild animals, birds and fish, and the more mysterious inhabitants of the deep. The 'command' given to human beings over all these created beings implies a responsible stewardship.

how majestic: This exclamation at the beginning and end of the psalm is not simply a detached glance at creation, but the profound amazement of a person responding whole-heartedly to the realisation of being loved at the heart of God's wonderful creation.

Suggestions for Praying with Psalm 8

Go out into a clear night sky, either physically or in your imagination. Now spend some time star gazing. Allow the simplicity of the psalm to inspire you as you admire these vast galaxies, and the mysterious and loving creator who has designed both them and you. Joseph Haydn's beautiful oratorio *The Creation* captures some of the exuberance of Psalm 8's outburst of praise.

Amazement indeed shapes and orders this entire psalm. It falls into two parts, both of which centre on the question, 'What are frail mortals … that you take note of them?' The first part speaks of the vastness of the universe, narrowing its focus as it arrives finally at frail humanity. The second part proceeds from these tiny lost beings, now strengthened in their experience of being much loved by God, and once more considers the universe of which humanity is its crowning glory.

We can pray this psalm both as individuals and within our Christian communities. Indeed it is a song of praise that can be articulated by all humanity. Together we bear collective responsibility for the wellbeing of our planet. Our amazement becomes the amazement of all who realize that they are not imprisoned in a blind and chaotic cosmos. We take courage from the belief that we are responsible stewards of a beautiful world, and that we can work to make a difference in how we exercise our 'command over the works of God's hands'.

Concluding Prayer

God of majesty and mystery,
your creative love reaches beyond the stars
and into the ocean depths.
The delicate imprints of your fingers
leave their signature in every corner of the universe,
no less than deep within the human heart.
Open my eyes to your presence in all of creation,
O beauty ever ancient, ever new.
Teach me to sing a song of gratitude
as you nudge me along the path of faithful love.
In the name of the Holy Spirit, my guiding light,
I make this prayer. Amen.

PSALM 19   *The Heavens Tell forth*

The heavens tell forth the glory of God,
and the firmament proclaims the work of his hands.
Day unto day pours forth speech,
and night unto night imparts knowledge.

No utterance at all, nor are there words,
not a sound is heard,
yet their echo resounds through all the earth,
and their words to the end of the world.

God has pitched a tent there for the sun.
It comes forth like a bridegroom from his canopy,
or like an athlete joyfully running his course.

From one end of the heavens it comes forth,
and its course runs to the other end.
Nothing can escape from its heat.

NOTES ON PSALM 19

Psalm 19 falls into two parts. These are quite different in mood and idiom, so it is possible that they were originally two separate psalms. The first part celebrates the glory of God as creator, while the second focuses on the law of God as perfect. Only the first part is explored here.

The heavens tell forth: Of themselves the heavens are incapable of speech. But contemplation of their beauty and vastness continually motivates human beings to tell forth the praise of God.

the firmament proclaims: The personification of the heavenly bodies continues in this next line. There is probably no difference in the poet's mind between the heavens on the one hand, and the firmament or sky on the other. The use of parallel expressions simply reinforces the imagery of this talking universe.

the work of his hands: Humanity, bowled over by the grandeur of the heavenly bodies, recognises them as created by God. The surrounding nations would have deified the sun, moon and stars, so the psalmist is making a clear theological statement here concerning the nature of Israel's unique God.

Day unto day ... night unto night: The entities of day and night likewise cannot speak, but their predictable and reliable sequence stirs humanity into speech in praise of their creator.

pours forth speech ... imparts knowledge: Just as day and night give way to each other in unceasing rotation, so too humanity's words of praise for God's glory pour forth incessantly like an endless stream.

No utterance ... not a sound is heard: Once again the poet reminds his audience that these wonders of creation cannot of themselves speak. Rather it falls to men and women to give them their voice through acknowledging their beauty as reflecting that of their creator.

their echo resounds: The paradox is that though these entities have no means of verbal communication, their silence is deafening, their echo resounds, and is heard by those attuned to God.

the end of the world: This refers to the extremities of the known inhabited world of that time.

pitched a tent: The remaining six lines concentrate on celebrating the splendour of the sun. The image of 'pitching a tent' would have had a special resonance for the early Christians, especially those of the Johannine community, since this is the language of John 1:14, 'and the Word became flesh and pitched his tent among us'.

like a bridegroom from his canopy: Continuing with further figurative language, the poet now compares the sun's emergence at dawn to that of a bridegroom emerging from the wedding tent or canopy.

like an athlete joyfully running: As day reaches its highpoint, running effortlessly like a fully fit athlete, this image radiates an ambiance of energetic celebration of God's creation.

From one end … to the other end: The sun, as the high point of God's creation of the heavenly bodies, reflects the omnipresence of its creator.

Suggestions for Praying with Psalm 19

The 'Canticle of the Sun' was composed about the year 1224 by St Francis of Assisi. Its opening lines mirror the mood of this psalm, with its focus totally on praise of God through the work of creation. Of the sun Francis wrote: 'Be praised, my Lord, through all your creatures, especially through my lord Brother Sun, who brings the day; and you give light through him. And he is beautiful and radiant in all his splendour! Of you, Most High, he bears the likeness.'

Like the psalmist, Francis gives a voice to the sun and the other heavenly bodies. Speaking on their behalf, he invites them to rejoice in their beauty, and in their reflected glory. Praying with this psalm invites feelings of praise and gratitude as you allow its poetic beauty speak to your experience.

Concluding Prayer

'Most high, all powerful, all good Lord!
all praise is yours, all glory, all honour, and all blessing'.
I pray with these words of St Francis
in admiration of your beautiful creation.
As I contemplate in awesome wonder
all the works your hands have made,
I thank you especially for the gift of Jesus Christ,
your Son and my Saviour.
I thank you that he pitched his tent among us
and showed us glimpses of your eternal beauty.
In the name of the triune God I make this prayer. Amen

PSALM 104   *The Architect of Creation*

Bless the Lord, O my soul.
O Lord my God, you are very great.
You are clothed with splendour and majesty,
cloaked in light as with a garment.

You stretch out the heavens like a curtain,
you lay the rafters of your dwelling on the waters,
you make the clouds your chariot,
you move on the wings of the wind.

You open up springs in the ravines,
running down between the mountains,
giving drink to every beast of the field.
The wild donkeys quench their thirst.

The trees of the Lord drink their fill,
the cedars of Lebanon that he planted.
In them the birds build their nests,
the stork has its home in the fir trees.

You have made the moon to mark the seasons,
the sun knows when to set.
You bring on darkness, and it is night,
when all the beasts of the forest go prowling.

Yonder is the sea, vast and wide,
with its creeping things beyond number,
living things both small and great.
All of them look to you in hope
to give them their food in due season.

When you hide your face, they are terrified.
When you take away their breath,
they die and return to their dust.
When you send forth your spirit, they are created,
and you renew the face of the earth.

May the glory of the Lord endure forever!
May the Lord rejoice in his works!
I will sing to the Lord as long as I live.
I will sing praise to my God while I have being.
Bless the Lord, O my soul! Hallelujah!

NOTES ON PSALM 104

Bless the Lord: Psalm 104 is a beautiful poem celebrating God as the architect of creation. Since it is quite long, what is presented here is a shorter version, focusing on the essence of the psalm. Its opening exhortation to bless God is identical to that of the preceding Psalm 103 (which is explored above in the section dealing with psalms of repentance).

my soul: This refers to the self as representing the totality of feeling, and is often, as here, a more emotionally charged alternative for a personal pronoun.

clothed with splendour and majesty: Before the dawn of creation, in the poet's imagination, God's essence was completely spiritual. Then, through the process of creation, God begins to clothe his spirit with various layers through which his infinite greatness might be grasped, within the limitations of humanity's capacity.

cloaked in light as with a garment: Just as a cloak envelops the one who wears it, God is enveloped in light. In the Genesis creation poem light is presented as the first of God's creative acts. In a symbolic yet paradoxical way, light is the first 'cloak' through which God's spiritual essence is both revealed and yet concealed.

You stretch out the heavens like a curtain: On the second day of the
Genesis creation narrative God creates the heavens. This creative act
is described poetically here as the drawing of a curtain across the vast
expanse of the skies.

you lay the rafters of your dwelling upon the waters: The ancient
Hebrews understood the heavens or the skies as containing a dome.
Reservoirs of water were stored above this dome. The poet portrays
God's mysterious upper chambers as resting on these waters. There were
openings in the dome which allowed the rains to fall in their seasons,
according as the floodgates of heaven were unbolted for this purpose.

the clouds your chariot ... wings of the wind: These are imaginative ways
of conveying how clouds and wind act as messengers of divine presence.

You open up springs in the ravines: The poet celebrates how God has
engineered earth's water supply as a marvel of technical ingenuity.

running down between the mountains: These rivers and streams are
channelled within protective banks so that they can flow freely and be
protected from the threat of stagnation.

giving drink to every animal ... wild donkeys: This effective water
supply system, valued in a region often lacking adequate reserves of fresh
water, served human needs, as well as those of animals, wild and tame.

The trees of the Lord ... that he planted: These lofty cedars are fashioned
in such a way that they need no human care; instead they are cared for
directly by the Lord.

the birds ... the stork: The cedars serve a vital function for the high-flying
birds, depicting yet again the poet's admiration of the genius of the
divine design.

the moon to mark the seasons: The psalmist now describes the creation of
the greater and lesser luminaries of Genesis 1:16. The moon is mentioned
first because in the biblical tradition night precedes day. The moon was
important in the Jewish calendar because the festivals were based on the
four-week lunar cycle.

the sun knows when to set: The precision of the sun's movements, both
in its daily orbit and annual cycle, was perceived to be more regular

than that of the moon, which seemed to change its appearance over the twenty-eight days in an erratic manner.

the beasts of the forest go prowling: In divine providence God has ordained that certain ferocious beasts hunt only at night, thus allowing human beings and their domesticated animals the safety of daylight.

the sea, vast and wide: The poet now turns to the creations of the fifth day (Genesis 1:17), and marvels at the vastness of the oceans and their numerous inhabitants.

All of them look to you in hope: This includes all land and sea creatures. Both groups instinctively hunt for appropriate food, though without knowledge of their creator. Only human beings are capable of appreciating and expressing gratitude to the ultimate provider of earth's abundant food.

When you hide your face: All living creatures depend on complex ecosystems for sustenance and survival. The psalmist celebrates how all of this is directly attributable to God.

When you send forth your spirit ... and renew the face of the earth: Christians down through the centuries have seen this verse as foreshadowing the coming of the Holy Spirit. This verse is often used in the liturgy at Pentecost.

May the glory of the Lord endure forever: The psalmist has now completed his overview of the work of creation. He is overwhelmed by the scope of God's accomplishment. In profound awe he prays that the Lord's glory may be forever praised. The text of Psalm 104 has been abbreviated for practical reasons, but readers should return to the Bible for the full range of the poet's celebration of creator and creation.

as long as I live: In recognition of all the wonders recounted in this psalm its author vows to sing praise to God as long as he lives, because afterwards it will be too late.

Bless the Lord: The psalm ends as it opened, with the invitation to bless the architect of creation.

Hallelujah! This is the first of many occasions in the remainder of the book of Psalms in which this acclamation occurs. See below at Psalm 150 where it occurs in abundance.

Suggestions for Praying with Psalm 104

This psalm celebrates God as creation's architect. It is a fine example of how the author is totally focused on God, who alone is worthy of the highest praise. In this psalm all of creation is presented as witnessing to the mystery of God, whose inner beauty and majesty can only be remotely imagined. St Ephrem, a fourth-century Syriac poet and theologian, spoke of how Nature and Scripture were the two primary avenues giving humanity some access to the indescribable mystery of God – Nature through our use of it, and Scripture through our reading of it. 'These are witnesses', he wrote, 'which reach everywhere, are found at all times, and are present at every hour'.

To gaze with the eyes of faith at trees and plants, at fruits and flowers, at birds and animals, all of them created by God, is nothing less than prayer. Patrick Kavanagh once wrote that it would take a life time to explore all the secrets of nature in one small field. David Attenborough would have agreed.

As you sit in your garden, or walk in a park, or stroll through a country lane, allow the music of this psalm to find its echo in your heart. By doing this you join in the vast canticle of praise of God that continues to be sung from biblical times to the present moment.

Concluding Prayer

Almighty God of creation and eternity,
within your providence we live and move and have
    our being.

Open our eyes to see your beauty
in all the details of our environment.
Lift our hearts to you in gratitude
for the luminosity of the stars
and for spiders and sparrows.
We thank you for the sun and the moon
which regulate our times and seasons.
We thank you for each and every person
who has enriched us on life's journey.
Most of all we thank you for your Word made flesh,
and for your Spirit of love and life,
God for ever and eternity. Amen.

PSALM 150 *The Great Hallelujah*

Hallelujah!
Praise God in his holy place,
praise him in his mighty firmament!
Praise him for his mighty acts,
praise him for his exceeding greatness!

Praise him with blasts of the horn,
praise him with lyre and harp!
Praise him with tambourine and dance,
praise him with lute and pipe!

Praise him with resounding cymbals,
praise him with loud-clashing cymbals!
Let everything that has breath praise the Lord!
Hallelujah!

NOTES ON PSALM 150

Hallelujah: The Hebrew words Hallelu-jah mean 'Praise ye Yah/Jah (a short form of Yahweh)' or 'Praise ye the Lord'. This invitation begins and ends this final psalm. It also sums up the entire book of Psalms, since praise lies at the heart of Hebrew prayer. Within this framework of Hallelujah there follows a series of eleven further acclamations of praise. They are arranged in a careful gradation which gives the composition its internal movement and climax.

Praise God: First of all, it is God in his mysterious essence who is to be praised, this God who is beyond all we humans can ever imagine or visualise.

in his holy place: God is to be praised initially in the temple sanctuary.

in his mighty firmament: Then God as creator of the entire cosmos is to be praised. This 'mighty firmament' would have represented for the Hebrews what today we call the entire universe, with all its galaxies and mysteries of outer space.

for his mighty acts ... for his exceeding greatness: The focus of praise now moves to God, as Lord of history. The motives for this praise lie in God's choice and deliverance of his people, all the divine love and care that the Exodus event embodied.

with blasts of the horn ... pipe: A detailed list of musical instruments now follows. It's like an orchestra where everyone is doing something. All possible human modes of bodily expression are evoked: wind and stringed instruments, resounding cymbals and the physical movements of dance. The psalm expresses one mighty celebration, in which there are no spectators.

Let everything that has breath: All animate creation is invited to participate in this final outburst of praise.

Suggestions for Praying with Psalm 150

Psalm 150 brings the collection of psalms to a close, thereby forming a fitting synthesis of the preceding 149 psalms. It marks the climax of a journey, when we as pilgrims finally learn to praise God fully and for his own sake. The original setting for Psalm 150 would have been the Jerusalem Temple, but with the passage of time, 'praising God in his holy place' takes on new and ever more profound meanings. For Christians this 'place' for praise is no longer the Jerusalem Temple. Rather, it is in Christ, as the doxology at Mass expresses: 'Through him, and with him, and in him, to you, O God, almighty Father, in the unity of the Holy Spirit, is all honour and glory, for ever and ever. Amen.'

On the basis of this Christian 'place of praise', the world of our time can also become a place of praise. There is no tiny flower, or blade of grass that does not sing its creator's praise. Renewed through Christ, our world can be transformed into a place of praise where it is truly right and fitting, always and everywhere to give thanks to the Father through his beloved son, Jesus Christ.

Praise expresses the marvel of not being the centre of the universe. It is shot through with the joy that there is someone greater than ourselves, someone who loves every person, someone who loves me. We are called to this praise in amazement and awe before the mystery of God, before the beauty and power of Jesus, the Word of God, and before the guidance of the Holy Spirit.

Concluding Prayer

Great God of endless mystery and beauty,
Creator God, Incarnate Son and Holy Spirit
I come before you to praise you.
I praise you in the immensity of the glittering night sky,
I praise you in the rhythm of the seasons and years,
I praise you in the beauty of art and music,
I praise you in the goodness and generosity of other
people.

Most of all, I praise you in your Son, Jesus Christ,
my strength, my fortress and my rock.
I make this prayer in the name of the triune God. Amen.

10 Voices of Prayer through the Centuries

Most people in the Judaeo-Christian tradition know something about the psalms. Psalm excerpts are used in various liturgies. Anyone who participates in church or synagogue worship knows that many psalms have been beautifully put to music. Almost everyone knows that 'the Lord is my Shepherd,' and some find encouragement at a funeral service in the words, 'Out of the depths, I call to you, O Lord' (Psalm 130:1).

So, given their quality of being ever ancient ever new, we may rightly ask where did these human voices of prayer and suffering come from, what was their experience of God, and why do they continue to reverberate through the centuries? There is no simple answer, but hopefully some of the reasons underlying their enduring appeal will have become a little clearer through exploring the foregoing chapters.

Psalms in the Hebrew Bible

There are 150 psalms in the Hebrew Bible assembled under the title of Psalms. These psalms came into being over a long period of history, perhaps five hundred years or more.

Authorship of the psalms is often attributed to David. But it is unlikely that he could have written any of them, since most of them reflect situations that arose centuries after David was dead. The tradition of Davidic authorship can be linked with the broader postexilic tendency to attribute blocks of writing to significant figures – the Torah to Moses, the Wisdom Literature to Solomon, and the Psalms to David. Davidic authorship would have been reinforced by texts such as 1 Samuel 18:10 and Amos 6:5, which describe

David as a musician, and by 2 Samuel 6:5, which notes how 'David and all the house of Israel were dancing before the Lord with all their might, with songs and lyres and harps and tambourines and castanets and cymbals.' Verses such as these portray David at his musical best, giving him a psalms profile down through the ages, which was alive and well in both Jewish and Christian medieval art.

The tradition of Davidic authorship was further cemented by the headings to many of the psalms. These superscriptions were added to various psalms at later stages, with as many as seventy-three psalm superscriptions linked explicitly to David. A further small number of psalms are variously linked to other persons or groups, with just twenty-four psalms left which carry no heading. In spite of these superscriptions, which are often omitted in modern translations, we simply do not know who 'wrote' the psalms. These anonymous authors remain invisible, as do the later editors who expanded the original compositions here and there. But their voices continue to reach across centuries, cultures and creeds to console and to challenge.

It has been said that poets give us a distance from events and from ourselves. They hold up a mirror in which we can safely see ourselves. These mirrors need to be clear and not distorted for any reason. A poet's strength lies in his or her determination to keep that mirror honest and rooted. The poets who composed the psalms certainly kept their mirrors real and rooted. That is why the realism and honesty of the psalms still touch our hearts today.

Arrangement of Psalms within the Book

The numbering of the psalms in the Hebrew text differs from that of the Greek version, which was the earliest translation of the Bible, and that used by the earliest Christian communities. Other renderings such as the Latin Vulgate followed the Greek tradition, and also some English translations, such as the Grail, which is currently used in the Catholic breviary and liturgy.

This difference in numbering is due to the fact that the Hebrew Psalms 9-10 and 114-115 are each featured as one psalm respectively in the Greek translation. By contrast, the Hebrew text for Psalms 116 and 147 are rendered as two separate psalms respectively in the Greek. This means that the numbering of both traditions evens out again for Psalms 148 to 150.

The Hebrew numbering is used throughout this book. The following chart illustrates the different numbering of each tradition.

Hebrew	Greek
1-8	1-8
9-10	**9**
11-113	10-112
114-115	**113**
116	114-115
117-146	116-145
147	146-147
148-150	148-150

The bringing together of the 150 psalms was a gradual process. Like the Torah with its five books, the Psalms were assembled into five 'books' or collections (Psalms 1-41; 42-72; 73-89; 90-106; 107-150). These collections are marked off from each other by the presence of a doxology or formula of worship in praise of God. The doxology is more or less similar in each case, with minor differences: 'Blessed be the Lord, the God of Israel, from everlasting to everlasting. Amen and Amen' (41:14). While some psalms or parts thereof may predate the Exile (597-539 BC), the final form of the book of Psalms may be as recent as the third century BC.

Ancient Israel at Prayer

The psalms show us ancient Israel at prayer. In contrast to much of the rest of the Hebrew Bible, which is concerned with revealing God's word from on high, or through the prophets, the psalms come from below. They are a mixture of human praise and petitions for help, cries from the depths and expressions of trust. The needs and concerns articulated in the psalms are very similar to ours, even if expressed in imagery that frequently differs from ours. Because the psalms were originally composed for liturgy they survived the centuries, being handed down from one generation to the next, not unlike some of our hymns.

Psalms would have been used most typically in temple worship, particularly during the three great pilgrimage feasts of Passover, Weeks and Booths. The Psalms of Ascent (120-134) would have been sung as the pilgrims 'lifted up their eyes' on approaching Jerusalem for these great feasts.

In the postexilic period, from the fifth century BC onward, synagogues began to emerge. Their main function was to be houses of prayer and study of the Scriptures in the local communities, in contrast to the Jerusalem Temple, which was the only place where animal sacrifices could be offered. As well as being integrated into temple liturgy, the psalms would have also formed an integral part of the prayer and study of the Scriptures in the synagogues.

The Psalms as Christian Prayer

Perhaps the most compelling reason for Christians to want to know more about the psalms is the fact that Jesus, during his life time, would have known and prayed them. As a young Jewish boy he would have learned them at home, and would have joined in reciting them in his local synagogue assemblies, as well as in the Jerusalem Temple.

It seems likely that the weekly synagogue liturgy would have consisted of Torah readings based on a three-year cycle. The Torah reading would have been followed by a reading from the Prophets (see Luke 4:16-17), which in turn would have been followed by a psalm. This could be one of the reasons as to why the book of Psalms in its final form contains one hundred and fifty psalms, arranged to accompany a three-year fifty-week cycle.

Since the first Christians were Jewish, and continued to frequent the synagogue (cf. John 9:22), it was understandable that they would have continued their practices of praying the psalms. We may have evidence for psalm singing in Colossians 3:16, 'Let the word of Christ dwell in you richly; teach and admonish one another in all wisdom; and with gratitude in your hearts sing psalms, hymns, and spiritual songs to God' (and perhaps also in Ephesians 5:19). It seems a reasonable presumption to understand 'psalms' in this context to refer to the book of Psalms. Christians today therefore stand in a long and noble tradition when they pray the psalms.

Index of Psalms

Numbering follows the Hebrew Bible, with the Greek equivalent, as appears in the Lectionary and in the Liturgy of the Hours, given in brackets (see page 137).